TENT
of HIS
PRESENCE

Louise Brock

Tent of His Presence
ISBN 1-929496-03-6
Copyright © 2000 by Louise Brock
Louise Brock Ministries
2551 West Orange Grove Road
Tucson, Arizona 85741

Published by Triumphant Publishers, Tulsa, Oklahoma

Cover Design by the Whisner Group, Tulsa, Oklahoma

Editorial Consultant: Phyllis Mackall, Broken Arrow, Oklahoma

DEDICATION

So many wonderful men and women of God have graced my life with teaching and examples of living in the "Tent of His Presence." But, one in particular challenged me to rise to a higher place. So I lovingly dedicate this book to my dear friend, Buddy Harrison, who now lives in the highest place . . . heaven.

CONTENTS

FOREWORD

I love the Holy Ghost. Why? Because He is everything to me that He has said He would be. He is my comforter, my close friend. He is the manifestation of the eternal, infinite, almighty God in my life.

When Louise asked me to write this foreword, I was honored because she is my dear friend and sister in Christ. Her ministry has richly blessed me for many years. I cherish her friendship and highly respect her as a teacher and woman of God. I look forward to our friendship continuing even into heaven where we will have lots more fun together in His presence.

In this book, Louise has richly laid out a path by which we can see and understand that God desires for us to dwell daily in His presence and be containers of His presence in this world.

As you read and re-read this book, let this knowledge become truth to you, for His truth will set you free to be the victorious believer the Lord has called you to be.

May this book bless you as it has blessed me. And may you come to know the freedom, joy, strength, and refreshing that comes from dwelling daily in Him.

Triumphantly Always in Christ,

Pat Harrison, Founder and President
Faith Christian Fellowship Int'l Church, Inc.

CHAPTER 1

THE MANIFESTED PRESENCE OF GOD

I'm a fourth-generation tongue-talker. My great-grandmother got filled with the Holy Spirit and spoke in tongues before Azusa Street, so I've been around this for a long time.

God is doing unusual, wonderful, and glorious things today. He is preparing us to reap the end-time harvest, and He has assigned a role in it to each of us.

In 1981, God used me to start a church in Tucson, Arizona, where I'm from. We started with seven people, and now we have about 2,000. My oldest son, Bruce, is the pastor.

Two years ago, God began to call our whole congregation into a supernatural season of repentance. It seemed like every sermon, every prophetic word, and everything else that came from God was about repentance. After about a month of this, I said, "Dear God, I don't have anything else to repent for. I'm having to search for something to repent for."

One Wednesday evening, God said to me, "I want you to repent for the sins of this church."

I said, "Father, this is a good church. I don't know what to repent for."

He said, "You're the founder of this church, and I'm going to show you some things."

Do you know what our sins are? He showed me they are sins of attitude and acts of omission, where we don't do what we know the Holy Spirit wants us to do.

Refreshing and restoration always follow repentance. Out of that deep season of repentance, God led me into seeking His face.

I began to study subjects that God dealt with me about, including the manifested presence, seeking His presence, preparing for His presence, being perfected in His presence, and so forth.

HABITATION, NOT VISITATION

God said to me, "Louise, I desire a habitation with My people, not a visitation. I have visited people for centuries, but I want to live with My people. This was My thought from the beginning of time. I made a place, a garden, and put man in the middle of that garden, because I have always wanted a family to live with, not just visit."

And He said, "You human beings have understood visitation quite well. Visitation is cyclical. You go up in revival and down in defeat; up in revival and down in defeat.

"When you come to the realization that I desire a habitation, the cyclical condition ceases, and your life is on an even course, because you know consciously that I am living in the midst of you both individually and corporately."

Because God desired a habitation, not a visitation, He made the Garden of Eden for Adam and Eve, and He lived there with them until they sinned. The Bible says in Genesis 3:8, "And they [Adam and Eve] heard the voice of the Lord God walking in the garden in the cool of the day...."

We get the impression that God came down to visit them only in the cool of the day, but "cool" has nothing to do with the time of day or the temperature. It's the word *ruach*, which means "spirit." God wasn't just visiting them; He was living with them

— and He came down to talk to them in the spirit of the day.

GOD'S PRESENCE WILL NOT DWELL WITH SIN

Our study of the presence of God begins in Genesis with the story of how Adam and Eve sinned. After they sinned, they "...hid themselves from the presence of the Lord God amongst the trees of the garden" (Genesis 3:8). This verse is the first time the word "presence" is used in the Word of God. "Presence" means a face-to-face encounter.

The first thing we recognize here is that God's presence will not dwell with sin! He absents Himself when sin is in the camp.

As we continue to lay this foundation, let's look at Genesis 4, where Adam and Eve were driven from the garden. God's presence came down to visit them. He could no longer live with them, because sin was there. Then they had to come back into the presence of God around sacrifices and altars to cover their sins. Cain offered the wrong sacrifice and then killed his brother, Abel, in a fit of jealousy. Verse 16 says, "So Cain went away from the presence of the Lord, and dwelt in the land of Nod [wandering], east of Eden." He was driven from the presence of God because of the sin in his life.

ENOCH: A YEARNING HEART

In Genesis 5, we find a hungry heart born out of the godly line of Seth. His name was Enoch. Enoch got tired of just visiting with God. He wanted to live with God, so one day when he was out walking and talking with God, God took him home "...and he was not; for God took him [home with Him]" (verse 24). This is another indication that God has always desired to live with a family. God loves families.

Consider this: God started with a family, not a church!

I was sharing this thought with a pastor friend recently, because my two sons work with me in ministry. Although God is not into nepotism, He is into families. In Old Testament days, families were called "tribes."

After Enoch went to be with the Lord, we come to the time when mankind got worse and worse and worse. In Noah's day, God was still coming down to Earth to visit men — in chapters 6 through 9 we find Him talking to Noah — but He was not living here among men.

GOD'S MAN OF FAITH

In Genesis 12, we read where God found a man who was a moon worshipper. His name was Abram. God called him out of Ur of the Chaldees, saying, "Come with Me, because I am going to bring you to a certain land, and I am going to make you the father of many nations. I am going to give you millions of seed or descendants, because I am looking for a family with whom I can live."

God never wanted the separation that came between Him and man, so He found this man of faith, called him into the land of Canaan, and you know the rest of Abram's awesome, wonderful story.

Abram became a pilgrim, settled in Canaan, and he and Sarai went through a terrible time trying to have a child. God changed their names to Abraham and Sarah. Finally they had the child of promise, Isaac.

God came and visited with the patriarchs Abraham, Isaac, and Jacob around altars and wells as these men presented themselves to Him; but, again, it was always a visitation, not a habitation.

In the last chapters of Abraham's life, when He cut the covenant with God, God said, "Now, Abraham, I'm going to tell you something. For your people to get numerous enough to inhabit all the square miles of this land, they must have many children, so I'm going to put them in the incubator of Goshen. They're going to live down there in Egypt and serve a hard Pharaoh. The first 30 years won't be so bad, but the remainder of the 400 years will be terrible." (See Genesis 15:13-16.)

THE TERRIBLE YEARS OF GOD'S SILENCE

What was awful was that for the 430 years between Genesis and Exodus, we don't have a written account where God ever came down to visit His people! The first 30 years, the children of Israel served under a good Pharaoh. The last 400 years, they suffered oppression under slavery.

During those 430 years of absolute silence, there was no prophetic voice standing on the hills screaming out God's words to His people. There were no priests standing in the gap between God and His family. And there was no audible or visual demonstration of God's presence.

Keep that in mind, because there were another 400 years of silence between Malachi and Matthew, when again God had absolutely nothing to say to mankind that is recorded in the Word of God. These seasons of silence occur when people reach a place of absolute sin, and God is no longer with them.

At present, the Church has been experiencing some of this silence. Some say that faith is at an all-time low, and not many powerful words have been prophesied recently.

However, the good news is, as soon as we

enter seasons of repentance, God comes on the scene, and once again powerful voices speak out God's will for us.

THE HEART OF A HEBREW

In Exodus 2, God found a righteous man named Amram from the tribe of Levi. His wife was named Jochebed, and they had a wonderful little baby named Moses. Deep within Moses, God birthed the heart of a Hebrew deliverer.

The oppression of the children of Israel was so severe, Pharaoh wanted to kill all the Jewish boy babies. Pharaoh was living off the slavery of almost 3 million Jews, yet he wanted to stop them from reproducing by killing their male children! There was something terribly wrong with Pharaoh's thinking!

The baby Moses, whose parents had placed him in a basket, was fished out of the river by Pharaoh's daughter, and he became Pharaoh's grandson by adoption. He was raised in all the culture, education, and riches of Egypt. He attended their war college. He wore a pointed cap and a little pointed beard, and he looked just like Pharaoh — but underneath all the finery of Egypt beat the heart of a Hebrew! Moses had a call on his life to be a deliverer.

When Moses was 40 years old, he saw a Hebrew slave being beaten, and he killed and buried the man's oppressor. I don't think Moses had murder in his heart. I think it was an accident, but he got caught because some people witnessed the murder — some fellow Hebrews!

Acts 7 tells us Moses assumed the Jews would know that he was sent to them. But when you get out of your season, no one is going to recognize your gift, and you're going to fall flat on your face.

I've got a lot of "dead Egyptians" from things

I've tried to do that weren't in God's season. I've birthed a lot of Ishmaels, too, because I get these great ideas — but they're not always God's ideas.

God has set me over 13 states as the regional director of Faith Christian Fellowship. Many people think the only way they can serve God is behind a pulpit, but there are a million other ways to serve God.

I frequently have to clean up messes made by people who thought they were called to do something, but they really weren't.

Let me tell you something. You can pray and fast yourself into a bag of bones, but if the gifts of God are not there for that call, you may as well forget it and go have a steak!

MOSES: A MAN OUT OF SEASON

So Moses thought he was called to be the Jews' deliverer, but he was out of season by 40 years! He ran for his life to the backside of the desert, a fugitive from justice. Here was a man who was in line to be the next Pharaoh, but he had to live in the wilderness for the next 40 years.

I take scholars' tours to Israel almost every year, and much of that land really is a wilderness. Once I was riding in an Egyptian bus with Lester and Louise Sumrall. It was stifling, flies were everywhere, and the food was terrible.

Just before we got to the border of Israel, Lester turned to me and said, "I don't know why anyone wants to fight over this. We ought to just give it to them!" I agreed.

Moses was out there on the backside of the desert taking his sheep round and round Mount Horeb, which is also called Mount Sinai. It was rocky, it was dirty, and he was unhappy. He had married a woman named Zipporah, a daughter of Jethro, the priest of Midian. She lived in their tent back at their encampment, and they had two children, but they had little else in common. Moses probably spent a lot of time with the sheep to avoid her.

By the time Moses was 80 years old, he had no hope and no vision. He was just wandering around out there in the wilderness, trying to scratch a meager living out of those sheep. At age 80, he was still working for his father-in-law. And he'd done this for 40 years! I can't think of anything worse.

GOD BREAKS HIS SILENCE

Poor old Moses was walking around tending those sheep when all of a sudden something happened on Mount Horeb, that mountain he'd been around hundreds of times.

After 430 years of silence, God spoke! A Voice spoke out of a burning bush. The Voice knew Moses' name. That would get your attention!

Jesus talked to a tree, and Moses talked to a bush. Moses said to the bush, "You know my name?"

The Voice from the bush replied, "Yes, you're Moses. Take off your shoes, for you are standing on holy ground" (Exodus 3:5).

Moses knew it was the voice of God. This supernatural encounter with the Godhead was an epiphany for him. As Moses stood before that burning bush, God began to commission him. He said, "Moses I'm going to send you back to Egypt. I have heard the cries of My people. I have seen their oppression. I promised your great-great-grandfather that they would come out of Egypt."

It was God's plan for the Jews to go down to Egypt, because 70 people were not enough to drive out all the tribes in Canaan and inherit the Promised Land. So God put them in this incubator for 430 years, and in those 430 years in Egypt, the Jews grew in number from 70 to about 3,500,000 persons!

Now they were numerous enough to drive out all the Hivites, Perizzites, Jebusites, and Canaanites with God's help. Just as their oppression got worse and worse, God came on the scene and sent Moses to deliver them.

God told Moses, "I'm going to send you back to Egypt to set My people free. They are numerous enough now for Me to bring them out of their Goshen captivity and into the Promised Land, where they can have everything their great-grandfather was promised."

God then said to Moses what He had once told Gideon, "I've heard their cries and seen their oppression. Now Moses, you mighty man of valor, rise up, go back to Egypt, and lead those people out!"

MOSES' DOUBTS

Moses replied, "Who are You talking to? Have you read my resume? I'm a murderer, a fugitive from justice. I'm in a horrible marriage. I'm 80 years old, and I'm still working for my father-in-law. I haven't preached a sermon in the 40 years I've been out here in the wilderness. I don't even have any sermon outlines left, so how could I go back there and preach? No one will listen to me!"

Then he added, "Have you checked in my tent, God? Zipporah doesn't like my religion. She thinks it's a bloody religion. We haven't gotten along well. Zipporah will fight everything I try to do. Besides that, You know my career died, and all my dreams have died. I'm not prepared for this assignment."

Moses was a hopeless person at that point, and

God began to deal with him. God said, "Moses it's not who you are, it's who I Am. Go back and tell the children of Israel that I Am, I Am. I Am has sent you. Then go to Pharaoh and tell him to let My people go. He won't do it without resistance, but I'm going to bring your people out to bring them into the inheritance I'm going to give them. So you do exactly what I tell you to do."

FAMILY, FAMILY, FAMILY

Moses still protested. He said, "But God, I don't even speak well. I stutter a lot. All I'm used to talking to is sheep."

God replied, "That's all right. I'll let your brother, Aaron, go with you and be your mouthpiece." Family, family, family!

I've been an Old Testament scholar since I was a child, and I can see all of this as in a video. I can see Moses going back home, opening the tent flap, and saying, "Hi, Zipporah. You'll never believe what happened to me today."

And she says, "No, probably not."

He begins to tell her about a bush on fire on Mount Sinai. Then he adds, "And a Voice spoke to me out of that bush, and guess what, Zipporah? God called me into the ministry!"

Zipporah replies, "What did you drink for lunch? God hasn't spoken in more than 400 years. What do you mean He called you?"

Moses says, "Yes, He called me to the ministry — to a deliverance ministry and a traveling ministry. So pack up, sweetheart, and get on your donkey, because we're headed for Egypt." She reacted all over the place.

THE RIGHT SEASON FOR DELIVERANCE

You remember the story. Moses went down to Egypt. After a long siege of plagues, God used this man to deliver His people.

It was the same call Moses had had all along, but now it was the right season.

It was the same anointing, but now it was the right season.

It was the same understanding, but now it was the right season.

God said, "Moses, I wanted a family. I desired a habitation. I love these people so much, I wanted to live with them. I want you to bring them out." I love God for adding, "Moses, we're not going to bring them out sick, broke, or depressed."

These Jews were slaves who had been crying, bawling, and squalling to God. Moses told them what to do, and they came out of slavery. Psalm 105:37 tells us that there wasn't a sick or feeble person among them, and they came out with the silver and gold of Egypt, which was a major world player at that time.

SATAN'S WORST NIGHTMARE

In one 24-hour period, Almighty God took the finances of the wicked and gave them to the righteous through a powerful act. And He's getting ready to do it again!

After all the terrible plagues God sent to Egypt, Pharaoh finally relented. When his own firstborn son died, he said, "Get out of my face!"

We're going to get so strong and take so much of the devil's wealth, he's going to say, "Get these people out of here! Get them out of my face!"

We're going to become strong and wealthy, and

we're going to reap the harvest and get billions of people saved. Satan's worst nightmare is a rich Church that loves God more than things — a Church that sees the possibilities of the harvest and knows that with God's help they will reap it correctly and efficiently. We give the devil headaches, because he is defeated, and God has a plan to take the wealth of the sinner and give it to the righteous — not to the stingy righteous but to the righteous who have a vision.

God doesn't care if you have boats and cars; God cares whether your heart is in the harvest. That's what He wants. He's still looking for a family. I'm so glad I'm part of the family of God!

DELIVERED INTO THE HAND OF GOD

I love this story of the Exodus. When the Jews escaped from Egypt, Moses took them right back to Mount Horeb or Sinai, where he'd had the encounter with God. He told them, "Folks, this is an important place to me. There's a memorial here, because this is where God spoke the word of deliverance to me about you."

It was at this point that the Jews began to understand that they weren't just delivered from bondage; they were delivered into the hand of God.

From Horeb to Canaan is normally an 11-day journey, but it took the children of Israel 40 years! I imagine the women went nuts. They had all this money from spoiling Egypt, but now they were wandering around in a wilderness where there wasn't even a Wal-Mart!

The historian Josephus tells us they built little wooden chests to contain all the jewelry, coins, silverware, linens, and other wealth they had taken out of Egypt.

The people set up their tents in ranks according to tribes. After the women got through their chores at night, putting the kids to bed and washing the dishes while the men "spat and whittled," these women went nuts. They'd run their hands through their coins and lament, "When — when — when are we going to get to spend this money?"

Someone probably suggested, "Canaan is just a few days' journey. They've got malls there, and we can have fun." I say it took them 40 years to reach Canaan because men won't stop and ask for directions, so they just went around and around that same old mountain!

Finally God said, "Get with it, Moses. These people are going to rot out here. We've got to do something."

GOD MARRIED ISRAEL

Moses brought the people out of captivity and led them to Mount Sinai, the mountain of God. Exodus 19 is a pivotal chapter in the Old Testament and the whole history of the Jewish people. This is the chapter where God married Israel — 3,500,000 people! "Moses," He said, "you have come up with Me on this mountain many times. I have manifested Myself to you and have allowed you to see My splendor and My glory. You have talked to Me, and I have given you direction. But I desire a family — not just you — to be intimate with. Now I want to expose these 3,500,000 people to My presence. I don't want you to have to tell them about it secondhand; I want them to know My presence.

"So I want you to bring them to this mountain. I'm going to talk to them just like I talk to you. Tell the people to bathe, wash their clothes, refrain from marital relations, and come to the mountain of God, because I am going to come down and marry them!

"Draw a big circle in the sand around the mountain, and tell the people not to cross that circle. When My presence is there, it's going to be awesome. Don't let the beasts cross the line, either, because they would be incinerated by the power of My presence. I want perfect order."

God was so excited. He said, "I want to gather My people around Me. You are My special people. You are a peculiar people. I've called you to Myself. I want you to live in My presence, for now I am going to marry you!" From then on, God is called *ishi*, or husband. He is the husband of Israel!

And from Exodus 19 through the minor prophets, every time Israel backslid, she was called the adulterous wife of God. New Testament believers, the Church, are the Bride of Christ; but Israel is still the wife of God — because God has never divorced Israel!

They are adulterous now, but a group is returning to God and to the land of Israel, and they will get a chance to become the faithful wife of God once more.

THE MARRIAGE CEREMONY

Exodus 19:1-6 shows us this marriage ceremony.

In the third month after the Israelites left the land of Egypt, the same day they came into the wilderness of Sinai.

When they had departed from Rephidim and had come to the wilderness of Sinai, they encamped there before the mountain.

And Moses went up to God, and the Lord called to him out of the mountain, Say this to the house of Jacob, and tell the Israelites:

You have seen what I did unto the Egyptians, and how I bore you on eagles' wings, and brought you to Myself.

Now therefore, if you will obey My voice in truth and keep My covenant, then you shall be My own peculiar possession and treasure from among and above all peoples; for all the earth is Mine.

And you shall be to Me a kingdom of priests, a holy nation....

After this talk of marriage, God began to give the children of Israel instructions, starting in chapter 20. He was addressing former slaves who had seen only a little of His power at work.

They had seen the plagues that tormented the Egyptians, but those plagues hadn't come near their camp. They had seen the firstborn in Egypt die, but their firstborn did not die. And they had seen the waters of the Red Sea literally stack up to allow them to walk across on dry land.

I have a vivid picture of this. Can you imagine the fish in the Red Sea swimming along one second and the next they were paralyzed in this gelatin, and they had to wait until all those people marched by on dry land before they could resume swimming.

The children of Israel saw the Egyptian army drown in the Red Sea once they got across safely. Then they experienced the miracles of the cloud shading them from desert heat by day and the pillar of fire warming them by night.

GOD'S PROVISION

They saw "bagels" on the ground every morning, and they asked, "What is this?" It was called "manna," and it was God's way of providing food for them.

I've been telling Christians not to get excited about Y2K. It sounds to me like the Tribulation. I don't know how you feel, but God has not reserved me for wrath, so I'm going up with the first load!

All my life, I've hated camping out. My dad hunted, fished, and bought tents and sleeping bags for us. He tried every bribe in the world, because I was his only daughter, and he wanted me to love camping — but I always hated it. My idea of "roughing it" is slow room service!

When I was talking to God about Y2K, I said, "It sounds like tribulation and camping out, and I don't believe I want to stay here. God, You put bagels on the ground for the Jews, and You love us in the same measure, so You could put steaks and hot rolls on the ground for us." (I don't see any of us looking very hungry anyway.)

THE FEAR OF GOD

> The third morning there were thunders and lightnings, and a thick cloud upon the mountain, and a very loud trumpet blast, so that all the people in the camp trembled.
>
> Then Moses brought the people from the camp to meet God; and they stood at the foot of the mountain.
>
> Mount Sinai was wrapped in smoke, for the Lord descended upon it in fire: its smoke ascended like that of a furnace, and the whole mountain quaked greatly.
>
> As the trumpet blast grew louder and louder, Moses spoke, and God answered him with a voice.
>
> **Exodus 19:16-19**

When God started to descend upon Mount Sinai, the people in the camp didn't have a clue about what was happening, and they began to tremble. They backpedaled as fast as they could away from that circle Moses had drawn in the sand.

They were in the midst of thunder and lightnings, an earthquake and a volcano shaking the ground. Thick smoke covered everything, and they heard a loud trumpet blast, but no one could see the a man blowing the trumpet! It scared them to death!

In the next chapter, they said, "My God, this is too awesome for us! Moses, if you don't mind, you go up to God and come back and tell us what He said. We don't believe we want to know God so well."

I love this part. I think God probably smiled, backed off, and said to the angels, "I was so eager to get them out of captivity and into My presence, I overdid it, didn't I? I wanted them out of Egypt. I wanted to marry My people. I wanted to hold them to My bosom. I wanted to make a family. I don't want a visitation, I want a habitation, and I've scared them to death."

GOD WANTS A HOUSE

"I'm going to have to build a place where My people can come into My presence and I won't scare them. I'm going to build a tabernacle just like My people live in." They lived in little tents made out of animal skins.

Exodus 25:8 is the first record in God's Word where He asked man to build Him a house. He said, "Let them make Me a sanctuary, that I may dwell among them."

God wanted His presence to be with His people all the time, and now He was married to them. God said, "Moses, in order for Me to become their God-husband, or *ishi*, I must veil Myself off from My people in My tabernacle, because My splendor, majesty, and power overwhelm them — but I'll still be with them.

"They saw Me take the Red Sea apart and let them walk across on dry land. They saw Me in the cloud that covered them in the daytime, and they saw Me in the pillar of fire by night.

"They saw Me in the manna and the quail every day and knew that I was going to feed them; they saw Me in the water that went with them everywhere they went. They saw Me in their clothes not wearing out; and they saw Me in their physical condition never deteriorating. They saw Me in all these miracles.

"They saw portions of My glory. But when I really want to get close to them and become intimate with them, it scares them. Therefore, I'm going to dwell in this sanctuary, this tent of skins, behind the veil."

In Exodus 25:21, God called Moses back to Him and gave him the plans for the tabernacle and the ark of the covenant. He also gave him priesthood instructions and sacrificial instructions so the people would know how to come into His presence.

AN INTIMATE MEETING

In verse 22, He said, "There I will meet with you and from above the mercy seat, from between the two cherubim that are upon the ark of the testimony, I will speak intimately with you of all which I will give you in commandment to the Israelites." Notice the important phrase "I will speak intimately with you."

So the people began to build the ark and create the candlesticks and the furniture that were to go inside what we call the tabernacle of Moses.

But during this period, the people severely tried

God's patience and Moses' patience as well. Between chapters 25 and 33, Moses went up into the presence of God and stayed there while God visited him and gave him instructions.

We don't know everything God told Moses while he was in His presence. However, Moses couldn't live indefinitely on the mountain; he had to come down eventually to pastor the people. When God visited His people, He was always present in what they could see in the pillar, the cloud, and so forth — but He still wanted to come down and dwell with them.

Remember, the children of Israel who lived under the Old Covenant were not "new creations" who had God dwelling in them.

CHAPTER 2

ENTERING THE MANIFESTED PRESENCE OF GOD

We, too, have known God in provision, protection, and direction. We, too, have known Him in marvelous things.

We have seen the cloud and the pillar of fire. We have known Him in the water of the Holy Spirit. We have known Him in divine healing. We have known Him in all these characteristics.

However, provision, protection, and direction do not encompass all the manifested presence of God; they are simply facets of it.

But now God is getting ready to bring us into the Holy of Holies — into His inner sanctuary — and we are going to be so infused with His glory, we are going to go from glory to glory to glory as new creations!

The Church is about to walk into the manifested presence of God! His presence is going to live with us in a habitual dwelling that is greater than any dimension we have ever experienced before.

We are about to walk into the very character and nature of Almighty God!

God is looking for a family in this new millennium to whom He can manifest His power in a greater dimension than He has ever done before. That's us — the Church — and we're not going to pull back.

Moses, the pastor of the children of Israel, went to the top of Mount Sinai, and God inundated him with His glory and His presence. When Moses came down from the mountain, he had to place a veil over his face, because his face was literally shining with the glory of God!

That glory was seen externally on Moses. Because he was not a new creation, as we are under the New Covenant, he had to be bathed on the exterior with the glory of God. That glory is on the *inside* of us.

Part of the reason why Moses wore a veil over his face was to keep the people from seeing that the glory would fade. Paul referred to that in Second Corinthians 3:7: "Now if (the ministration of the Law,) the dispensation of death engraved in letters on stone, was inaugurated with such glory and splendor that the Israelites were not able to look steadily at the face of Moses because of its brilliance, (a glory) that was to fade and pass away."

After the glory faded, Moses had to go back up on the mountain and get in the presence of God again. However, we who are in the New Covenant go from glory to glory. We're in ever-increasing glory. We are more filled with the glory of God than Moses was, and the glory does not dissipate in us.

DISCOURAGEMENT AND IDOLATRY

Exodus 33 is another pivotal chapter. One day Moses went up on the mountain, and he was gone longer than usual. The people down below began to mumble, grumble, and complain. There was a cloud up on the mountain, and they didn't know where Moses was. They thought he might have died.

Then they looked at Aaron, the assistant pastor, and said, "Our pastor has gone, and we don't know if he's ever coming back to us and his wife and kids. Look at this mess down here! Moses hasn't led us into the Promised Land. We're still out here in the wilderness, and now what are we going to do?

"We had it better in Egypt, because we had gods we could see. All we can see is this mountain that quakes, shakes, and belches smoke. We hear the sound of the shofar, but we can't see it. The mountain is covered in smoke. Let's build a calf to worship."

So the people gave their golden jewelry and coins to Aaron, saying, "Make us a calf, an image of Baal, that we can see and worship."

Can you believe this? These people who'd been out in the wilderness for months, living by the provision of God, were willing to trade divine provision for social security!

Moses had just received the tablets of the Law and was heading back to camp. Joshua, who was with him, said, "I hear the sound of singing and dancing. They're having some kind of a party down there. I wonder what's going on?"

THE MYSTERIOUS GOLDEN CALF

I love this. Moses got to the camp, saw the golden calf, walked up to Aaron, the associate pastor he'd left in charge of the congregation, and demanded, "Aaron, what's this idol doing here?"

"I don't know, Moses," Aaron replied. "The people got so discouraged because you were gone so long on your vacation, they didn't know what to do. They started bringing me all this jewelry. I threw it in the fire, and out jumped this golden calf! They've been worshipping it ever since."

And Moses said, "You jerk, we left idolatry and all that junk in Egypt!"

At this point, I think Moses was so angry, he looked toward heaven and said, "God, kill them all! Cremate them on the spot!"

God replied, "Moses, we can't kill all of them. If we do, the nations around you will say that I wasn't able to bring you out of Egypt to bring you in to Canaan.' We can't do it, Moses. Let's kill just a few." So He incinerated a few that day.

As always, God and Moses didn't get mad on the same day. It's a good thing they didn't, or the whole congregation would have died in the wilderness! Either Moses was interceding with God or God was interceding with Moses.

A few days later, God got mad and said, "Get out of the way, Moses. I'm going to strike them all with lightning and incinerate them on the spot!"

Moses said, "God, wait a minute! Remember, You said that if we killed them all, people in other nations would say You weren't able to bring us in." So God relented and only killed a few.

GOD KEEPS HIS PROMISE

Exodus 33:1 says, "The Lord said to Moses, Depart, go up from here, you and the people whom you have brought from the land of Egypt, to the land which I swore to Abraham, Isaac, and Jacob, saying, To your descendants I will give it."

Then He added, "I will send an angel before you, and I will drive out the Canaanite, Amorite, Hittite, Perizzite, Hivite, and Jebusite. Go up to a land flowing with milk and honey...." (verses 2 and 3).

But notice the remainder of verse 3: "...but I will not go up among you, for you are a stiffnecked people! If I should come among you for one moment, I would consume you...."

The children of Israel had tried God's patience to the limit! He was willing to send His angel with them to the Promised Land — and He was going to keep His part of the bargain by giving them the land — but He was not going to go with them there!

When the people heard that, the Bible says they mourned (verse 4). Moses did not say anything.

MOSES' RESPONSE

I love this story about God's presence! God has given me great revelation on this chapter. When I delved into the ancient Hebrew, I began to see some things in Exodus 33:7:

> **Now Moses used to take [his own] tent and pitch it outside the camp, far off from the camp, and he called it the tent of meeting [of God with His own people]. And everyone who sought the Lord went out to [that temporary] tent of meeting, which was outside the camp.**

Again, this tent was not the Mosaic Tabernacle; it was Moses' personal prayer tent that he pitched outside the camp.

You, too, need to build a tent of meeting with the presence of God far off from the camp of your busyness, far off from the camp of your work place, far off even from the pressure of your ministry.

Put it "far off" — outside the camp and outside the busyness of your life. Then enter the tent of His presence and meet God face-to-face! When you leave, you will know that you were in the presence of God, and He has found a habitation in you.

But God will not interrupt you. You must take time to find that tent of His presence in your life. You must crave intimacy with the Father in the tent of His presence, or you will never become what God has for you.

The anointing lifts off of you as people make demands on your life. Therefore, place the tent of His presence outside of everything that is demanded of you in this life, and spend time in His presence.

It doesn't happen in a second or two. It takes time to shut down your mind and all the pressures that are in the soulish realm. It takes time to get into the tent of His presence and stay there — outside the camp.

IN HIS PRESENCE

When Moses went out to his tent of meeting: "...all the people rose and stood every man at his tent door, and looked after Moses, until he had gone into the tent" (Exodus 33:8).

And when Moses entered that tent of meeting with God, "...the pillar of cloud would descend and stood at the door of the tent, and the Lord would talk with Moses" (verse 9).

God's presence was always waiting for Moses. When you separate yourself from everything inside your camp, and you walk outside to that place where you meet with God in the tent of His presence, He will always be there.

God is more eager to talk to you than you are to talk to Him. But you must desire to be quiet and to be in that tent of His presence.

LETTING YOUR LIGHT SHINE

The pillar of the cloud of His presence will stand there, and God will talk to you. And everyone around you will see the evidence of His habitation with you.

When you become a worshipper who takes time to stay in the tent of God's presence, you will involve those around you. They will desire God's presence in their lives to a greater degree, because they will see it operating in yours.

As I look at some people, I desire for God to be

as real in my life as He is in theirs. They challenge me to know more of God.

As I stand and watch the pillar of the cloud descend to them, I say to myself, "I'm going to get a tent of His presence, and I'm going to learn some secrets of how to get in His presence."

In fact, it creates worship in other people's hearts when you abandon yourself to the presence of God. Verse 10 says, "And all the people saw the pillar of cloud stand at the tent door, and all the people rose up and worshiped...."

"And the Lord spoke to Moses face to face, as a man speaks to his friend. Moses returned to the camp, but his minister Joshua, son of Nun, a young man, did not depart from the [temporary, prayer] tent" (verse 11).

THE SECOND GENERATION

Moses was in his eightieth year, and Joshua was 40. I was reading this and meditating on it, and God said, "Louise, did you know that in every major project of mine, I always involve two generations? I use an older generation to begin the project, and I use the younger generation to finish it."

He continued, "I used Moses to bring the children of Israel out of Egypt, and I used Joshua to take them into the Promised Land. I used David to get all the money and the plans ready for the Temple, but Solomon built it.

"In the New Testament, Peter, James, and John walked with Me every day, and they were the pioneers of the Gospel, but I used Paul, Luke, and Timothy — the second generation — to write the Gospel for the Church.

"I've always had the Moses generation bring the people out and the Joshua generation bring them in.

The older generation cannot be done away with, because they know the boundaries. They understand the movings of the Spirit. They have been there, and they have seen it.

"The Joshua generation that rose up a few years ago was wrong. They wanted the Moses generation to die, but they need you. They need your experience. They need to know how to pray. They need to know how to intercede. They need to know how to groan in the Spirit. They need to know all these things that were taught by the generation before you.

"Moses needed Joshua. He need his vision, his energy, and his creativity. You need the Joshuas of your day. You need their energy. You are part of the Moses generation in this time. I charge you to build a tent of My presence and let the next generation come into your tent and stay on their faces until they know who I am."

I said, God, "I'll do it! I'll do it!"

I have made the decision to bring the tent of God's presence to the people and be part of the Moses generation. You are welcome to come into the tent, stay on your face as Joshua did, and drink of the presence of God.

The Moses generation is needed by the Joshua generation. You need my wisdom. It is not because I am so smart; it is just because I have lived so long, gone so many places, and seen so much. I have been in the Word for 60 years.

THE HARVEST GENERATION

So you need me — but, boy, do I need you! I need your enthusiasm, your drive, and your vision. I'm in the age category that dreams dreams, but you're in the age category that has visions. I need the Joshua generation!

We are in the greatest project of the last 2000 years — the harvest generation — and we need each other. Joshua made the decision to stay in Moses' tent, but did you notice that Caleb wasn't seen in Moses' tent?

Moses would go up on the mountain, get in God's presence, bring it down to that tent, and Joshua would stay there. I believe Joshua remained praying on the floor of that little tent because the presence of God was so weighty there.

When Moses had to go back out and pastor the congregation, I believe Joshua remained on his face on the floor of that tent, because he encountered God there. He realized the habitation of God was in that place, and he wouldn't leave.

I once asked God, "Where was Caleb?"

He said, "I'm glad you asked. Let Me show you something. Caleb was only interested in his family's inheritance, but Joshua was interested in the nation. People who stay in the tent of My presence are interested in the multitudes, not in what their families can get."

As Joshua waited on God in the tent, His presence burned out Joshua's selfishness. He had a heart for God, and he had a heart for the nation. He stayed in the presence of God — in the tent of His presence — in Moses' day, and later he led the nation into their inheritance.

Caleb only took the mountain of Hebron for his inheritance. Both were godly men, but there was a big difference in what they accomplished. To whom much is given, much is required.

MOSES' SURPRISING REQUEST

This was Moses' response to what God had said in the first four verses of Exodus 33:

...See, You say to me, Bring up this people; but You have not let me know whom You will send with me. Yet You said, I know you by name, and you have also found favor in My sight.

Now therefore, I pray You, if I have found favor in Your sight, show me now Your way, that I may know You [progressively become more deeply and intimately acquainted with You, perceiving and recognizing and understanding more strongly and clearly] that I may find favor in Your sight....

Exodus 33:12,13

God's presence is addictive! You can never get enough of the presence of God.

Moses had been on the mountain with God — he'd had many awesome encounters with God — yet here He was saying, "God, when You called me at the burning bush, You said I had found favor with You. You said You knew my name. You said You would go with me. I don't think I want to go with an angel. I want to know You better. Show me more of You."

Verse 13 concludes, "...And, [Lord, do] consider that this nation is Your people." God relented on the spot. Verse 14 says, "And the Lord said, My presence shall go with you, and I will give you rest." This is a key phrase!

TRUE SABBATICAL REST

True sabbatical rest is only found in the presence of God. You won't find it in sleeping late on Saturday morning, taking a vacation to Hawaii, keeping busy with activities, fulfilling the vision God gave you, or doing other godly things.

God told Moses, "In my presence you will have rest."

Pastors, there should never be any burnout in the ministry if you stay in the presence of God and draw on His strength. Where do you think Joshua got his strength? In the presence of God. There is rest in the presence of God!

The presence of God will give you the rest — the sabbatical, supernatural rest — you need.

Jesus said:

> **Take My yoke upon you, and learn of Me; for I am gentle (meek) and humble (lowly) in heart, and you will find rest — relief, ease and refreshment and recreation and blessed quiet — for your souls.**
>
> **For My yoke is wholesome (useful, good) — not harsh, hard, sharp or pressing, but comfortable, gracious and pleasant; and My burden is light and easy to be borne.**
>
> **Matthew 11:29,30**

I love this man Moses! He's a Jew, and he wants to argue. As the joke goes, if you've got two Jews, you've got three opinions. Moses said, "God, I just want to say that if Your presence doesn't go with us, we're not leaving here!"

God said to Moses, "Come on, Moses. Quit struggling with golden calves and unfaithful priests like Aaron. I'm going to take you into My presence. I'll live up to My Word. My presence will go with you, and I will give you rest."

Moses was ready to follow the cloud.

CHAPTER 3

GO WITH THE FLOW

My mother and daddy were both ordained with the Assemblies of God. My mother taught in the very first Assemblies of God Bible school in 1929 in Amarillo, Texas. It was called Shield of Faith. Daddy was one of the students. The only way he could graduate was to marry his teacher!

My father was a true apostle. He and my mother built 14 churches. My father has gone to be with Jesus. He is now in the presence of the Lord he loved so much. Mother is 92.

I have been in this Pentecostal move all my life. I remember, as a little bitty girl, seeing Aimee Semple McPherson coming down out of her apartment spotlighted with kleig lights, drum rolls, and all the drama of her persona. She taught Hollywood everything they know today.

She was the anointed of God; a tremendous woman. In my little mind, I thought, "My goodness, that must be God coming down those steps from Mount Sinai!" I didn't know it was just a woman receiving all this fanfare.

I played the organ for William Branham in his midwinter campmeetings. A. A. Allen was down the road only 70 miles. Jack Coe held meetings in Fort Worth when I lived in Waxahachie, Texas, and Gordon Lindsay was in Dallas.

I've seen all the "greats," but I'm here to tell you one thing: When the cloud moves, I move with it!

Don't stay in the last wave of God when the new wave breaks. Be willing to follow the cloud wherever it goes. Don't allow tradition, family, or pressure to keep you back when the cloud is moving.

THE NECESSITY OF GOD'S PRESENCE

Moses said in Exodus 33:15, "...If Your presence does not go with me, do not carry us up from here!"

In the next verse, Moses continues to plead with God, saying, "For by what shall it be known that I, and Your people have found favor in Your sight? Is it not in Your going with us so that we are distinguished, I and Your people, from all the other people upon the face of the earth?" (verse 16).

What makes your church different from the church down the road? The presence of God. They could move into the same presence you're in if they wanted it and knew how to get it.

Your church will be different from others if your pastor is committed to going on with God and if he uses whatever method and means it takes to go with God. In other words, if the cloud stays, your pastor stays, but when it moves, your pastor moves.

God's presence with you distinguishes you from all those who are still struggling with the benefits God has for them.

In God's presence there is no lack.

In God's presence there is no indecision.

In God's presence there is no illness.

In God's presence there is no lack of glory.

And in God's presence every need is met.

CHARACTERISTICS OF NEW WAVES

Don't be critical and judgmental about the new wave. Every new wave comes in with excessive demonstrations. Don't criticize it.

You may not like all the laughing, the shaking, the falling down, or the different kinds of worship. I don't understand all of it, either, and I've been around a long time. I've seen and heard it all — and if I stay around long enough, it will come around again.

Brother Kenneth E. Hagin reminds me of that regularly. He says,

"Aren't you glad we saw it once?"

I reply, "Yes, sir. I'm glad I saw it."

Let me tell you something: Don't touch the new wave and become critical of it. It will all even out, and God will accomplish His purpose. But if you get critical and judgmental, you won't be part of it, because you're not moving with the cloud.

Do you know who always oppresses the new wave? The old wave. They get suspicious and uncomfortable with the new things of God. For example, God is doing new things in music. Those in the new wave are not singing the same old songs. They don't even use hymnals — they read the words to songs off a screen on the wall!

GREEDY FOR GOD!

Moses didn't have a critical attitude. Look at him — he was greedy for God! I love that. He said to God in Exodus 33:18, "...I beseech You, show me Your glory."

This sounds redundant, doesn't it? After all, Moses was the man who had been up on the mountain with God! He was the man who had stayed on the mountain with God for 40 days without food or water! He was the man who had so much glory on him when he came out of the presence of God, he'd had to cover his face with a veil!

He was the man who had been in God's presence time and time again — yet he said greedily, "...I beseech You, show me Your glory." Why? Because the presence of God is addictive! Once you're there, you want more of God. When we press into God like that, it delights His heart!

God responded to Moses' request by saying, "...I will make all My goodness pass before you, and I will proclaim My name, THE LORD, before you; for I will be gracious to whom I will be gracious, and will show mercy and loving-kindness on whom I will show mercy and loving-kindness" (verse 19).

SAFE IN THE CLEFT OF THE ROCK

Then, in verse 20, God said something that sounds like a contradiction of verse 11, which says that God spoke to Moses face-to-face. Yet in verses 20 to 23, God said:

> ...You can not see My face, for no man shall see Me and live.

> And the Lord said, Behold, there is a place beside Me, and you shall stand upon the rock.

> And while My glory passes by I will put you in a cleft of the rock, and cover you with My hand until I have passed by.

> Then I will take away My hand, and you shall see My back; but My face shall not be seen.

Moses said, "God I just want more of you. I want to be enraptured and enfolded in your presence. Show me more of Your glory."

God replied, "Sure, Moses. I'll do that. Come and stand right here by Me in the cleft of the rock on the craggy face of this mountain. I'm going to put My hand over this rock and pass by, and you're going to see My backside."

GOD SHOWED MOSES CREATION DAY!

You see, Moses was alive to write Exodus, Leviticus, Numbers, and Deuteronomy — but Moses was not even born at the time of the Book of Genesis. God showed him His past!

As God walked in front of Moses, and Moses saw the backside of God, he saw creation morning! He saw creation day, when God created Adam and Eve! He saw the calls of Abraham, Joshua, and Joseph!

He saw those things now recorded in the Book of Genesis, and he wrote them, because while Moses was there in the presence of God, God showed him His past.

But He said, "You can't see My face, because you don't know the future. I will give you direction, but you cannot know the future. However, you can see My past and put it in a book and call it the book of beginnings. So Moses sat down and penned Genesis.

When God placed him there beside Him on the rock, and Moses began to see God's past, he said, "Oh, this is greater than I ever imagined!"

Let me tell you what reviewing God's past will do. It will make you comfortable with your future. It will literally give you revelation about your direction for the future.

AFTER YOUR MOUNTAINTOP EXPERIENCE

Moses craved God's presence more than his next drink of water. He wanted to remain in that glorified presence of God, but God will always require you to come out of His presence and go back down with the "turkeys."

You can soar like an "eagle" up there on the mountaintop, but God's presence is given to you for "fruit"; not to make you into some big, superspiritual "nut."

We find this principle in the New Testament, too. In Luke and Mark, you'll find where Jesus took Peter, James, and John with Him to the Mount of Transfiguration.

He didn't take them with Him because they were His favorites; He took them with Him because they were the troublemakers on His staff. He didn't dare leave them behind with the other nine to cause another mini-riot about who was the greatest and the most famous!

The disciples had an enormous spirit of competition among them, because many of them had been fisherman, and you know that golfers and fishermen fib about everything!

THE DISCIPLES' AMBITIONS

These guys were so competitive, they argued all the time. They were always fussing about who had the greatest ministry, who had the biggest tent, who had the largest mailing list, and who had been on television the longest.

They hadn't done anything yet, but they wanted to set up big evangelistic crusades. However, the local people didn't want them, and they would come back and complain, "Lord, they don't want us here. Let's call down fire from heaven and cremate the whole town!"

And Jesus would say, "Now that's a great way to spread the Gospel!"

He knew these boys. I think that's why He went away so often by Himself to fast and pray. He thought, "Dear God, did I get the right staff?" (I've prayed that prayer myself.)

Jesus didn't pray because He was overcome by

His mission; He was trying to get those 12 guys to work together as a unit, because they were going to become the foundation of the Church!

Remember, one of them, Judas, was a thief and a liar. He stole money and ended up committing suicide. When I think about Jesus' staff, I say, "Thank You, God. My staff is not so bad."

I love this story where Jesus took Peter, James, and John with him to the top of a mountain, and they went to sleep. Isn't that amazing?

ELIJAH AND MOSES MINISTER TO JESUS

Here came Elijah and Moses, supernatural apparitions, and they talked to Jesus about the very thing that was concerning Him: His demise.

They gave Him instructions about how He was going to die, be resurrected, and become the Lamb of God, the foundation of the Church.

All of a sudden, Peter rubbed his eyes, looked, and saw two guys from another world conversing with Jesus, his boss. And Jesus was so radiant, so covered with the presence of God, His raiment was glistening white.

Peter probably rubbed his eyes again and thought, "Goodness, this is really a strange sight," so he poked the other guys, and they woke up.

WHY GOD PUTS YOU TO SLEEP

Sometimes when God is about to do something absolutely spectacular, He will put you to sleep or make you comatose. He did this to Adam, or he would have been telling God how to make Eve.

God probably said, "You don't have a clue about what you need, Adam. I know, so go to sleep." When Adam woke up, he said, "Wow — look at this fox!" God did know best.

God also did this with Abraham when He was about to cut covenant with him. He had Abraham get everything ready, but when it came time for the actual covenant-making, God put him in a coma.

The presence of God was the burning torch in the furnace that walked between the pieces as God the Father and Christ Jesus the Son cut covenant with each other, Jesus being the representative Man for Abraham. God knew that Abraham couldn't mess it up at that point if he was in a coma.

PETER'S MEMORIAL CHURCHES

So Peter, James, and John were asleep when Elijah and Moses came on the scene with Jesus. Peter woke up and, as usual, his mouth went into gear before his brain did.

He said, "Boy, what a revival this is! The awesome presence of God is on this mountain. Let's never leave it. Let's build three churches up here and call them the Church of the Supernatural, the Church of the Superspiritual, and the Church of the Nerds!"

God said, "Hush, Peter. Listen to My Son. He's got the plan."

Jesus and these three disciples went down from the Mount of Transfiguration into a crowd where there was a little boy who had a demonic spirit that would throw him into the fire. The other nine disciples had not been able to deliver the boy.

When you come down from the mount of the presence of God into the valley of need, you are to meet the people's needs. You are to pour out the presence of God to the needy who are at the foot of the mountain. Being in the presence of God is not just to make you spiritual.

Moses wanted all the presence of God he could

contain, but he always had to come down from Mount Sinai eventually.

Pastors, you may think you have it rough, but you have never pastored three and a half million Jews like Moses did. They are the toughest people on the face of the earth!

MY WEALTHY JEWISH FRIEND

Several years ago, I had ministered at an International Convention of Faith Churches conference in Charlotte, North Carolina, and was on the last leg of my journey, flying from Dallas to Tucson, sitting in first class. Across from me was a Jewish man.

He was reading a magazine called Texas Monthly that had some information in it about television infomercials. An advertising company had just talked to me about an infomercial, so I was interested in it, but I was also tired. I kept hoping the man would lay the magazine down so I could ask to borrow it.

About 20 minutes outside of Tucson, I said, "Do you mind giving me the subscription card out of that magazine?"

He said, "No, I don't mind at all. Do you want to subscribe?"

I said, "Yes, I do, and I really want that issue, so I'm going to call and ask for it."

He said, "Well, I'll be happy to give you this one. I'll tell you what I'll do: I'll subscribe for you."

I said, "Well, aren't you nice!" (God does neat things like this for me all the time.)

He asked, "May I have your card?"

I said, "Sure." I gave him the card, and he started talking to me.

THE DIALOGUE BEGINS

He asked, "Do you live in Tucson?"

I said, "Yes, sir, I do."

He said, "What do you do?

I said, "I started a church in Tucson. I'm a Bible teacher, and I've just been preaching and teaching at a conference in Charlotte."

He said, "That's interesting."

I asked, "What do you do?"

He said, "I'm retired. Do you know where Canyon Ranch is?"

Canyon Ranch is the spa of spas. It's an enormous spa in Tucson that costs clients something like $10,000 a week.

He said, "I have a house, a casita, there."

A casita in Canyon Ranch is very expensive.

He added, "I've been coming out here for years."

I never gave him another thought.

My driver met me and took me home. That was on a Sunday.

GIFTS OF GRATITUDE

Tuesday, my dad and I returned from lunch at his favorite deli, and we walked into my office. It takes a lot to impress me, but I was really impressed. On my big conference table was a hotel-sized flower arrangement of roses, lilies, and so forth. People have sent me flowers before, but they were always much smaller arrangements. I thought, "Boy, they really appreciated my preaching at that meeting in Charlotte!"

I picked the card out of the arrangement, and it said, "Thank you for the conversation. I would really like to hear more about what you do." It was signed by the Jewish man, but I hadn't asked him for a card, so I didn't know his name.

I thought, "Who is this man? With those flowers, it's worth a call."

When I looked at the phone number, I realized, "That's the guy at Canyon Ranch." So I called the number and thanked him. I said, "I'm just over-whelmed! Those flowers are gorgeous."

He asked, "Could you have dinner with me?"

I said, "Sure." We agreed to meet at a certain restaurant. He drove up in his new Mercedes, and I was in my Lexus. I thought, "Well, God, there is more than one way to build your kingdom, and You've always used Jews!"

THE WOMAN PREACHER AND THE RABBIS

I began to talk to him about the Lord. After that, every time he was in town, he would invite me to dinner. Through him, I have met some of the justices on the Canadian Supreme Court, because they visit him in Tucson.

I've also met rabbis by the score. They know I'm an old Testament scholar, and they ask, "Where did you learn all this?" Then they want me to take them on my tours to Israel!

I prayed and prayed for my Jewish friend. He called me last week. He's got a little cancer on his nose, and he asked, "You got any more prayers?"

The Jews I've met argue a lot, but not with me. I've thought, "Moses, how did you pastor all these people?"

I kid the rabbis by asking, "How many people are in your congregation?" They'll tell me, and I'll say, "How in the world do you handle all of them?"

And they laugh. They're the ones who tell me Jewish jokes!

I asked one rabbi, "Have you ever read the Book of Exodus?"

He replied, "I know the Pentateuch by heart."

"Well, how many times did Moses fall on his face because the people were so ugly?"

He said, "I don't know, but that's how he got his flat nose!"

Isn't that a wonderful story? Here's this little old lady preacher, and I've been able to meet all these Jewish guys.

A MUSICIAN IN DISGUISE

I've got to share another story about airplanes that happened once when I was flying to Redding, California. At the airport, I saw a little guy wearing black pants, a black top, a hat, big black glasses, and a funny little denim scarf. I thought, "I wonder who he is?"

Wouldn't you know, he got on, put something in the overhead compartment, and sat right next to me! Three or four other guys dressed like him got on the airplane, and they talked to him respectfully. All of them had heavy accents.

I was reading a book, and I thought, "Lord, I don't want to talk to this guy. He's too weird!"

He said, "Do you live in Sacramento?"

"No, I live in Tucson."

"Why are you going to Sacramento?"

"So I can catch a ride to Redding."

"What are you going to do in Redding?"

"I'm going to preach." Usually that stops people. When they find out I'm a woman preacher, they want nothing to do with me. They move away from me and get their magazine out.

He looked at me and asked, "Preach?"

I replied, "What are you going to do in Sacramento?"

He said, "We have a gig."

"Well, that's what I have in Redding — a gig."

He said, "I'm from Argentina."

He then told me he is a famous Latin musician who lives in New York. He told me about his band and their gigs.

He said, "You see I'm dressed different."

I said, "Yes, you really are."

"It's a disguise."

I said, "It really works, because I sure don't know who you are."

"Do You Know Jesus?"

We had this wonderful conversation, and I began to talk to him in my household Spanish, because he's from Argentina. When he found out I was going to Argentina to do a pastors' conference, he started giving me a list of all the best restaurants, musicians, and places to visit in Argentina, even though I was only going to be there for 10 days.

I then asked him, "Do you know Jesus?"

He exclaimed, "I'm Catholic."

I said, "I don't care what you are; it's who you know."

He said, "I think so."

"Well, do you know His mother?"

He said, "Oh, yes, I know Mary."

"It's pretty important that you know her Son," I

pointed out.

My Spanish was not that good, and I did not have a tract in Spanish, but I promise you, I am going to learn how to lead someone to the Lord in Spanish.

The man told me that he lives in New York, and he is a widower. He was quite sad. He added, "I'm 66."

I said, "So am I."

And he exclaimed, "Mother of God!" and slapped his head.

Then we started talking about age, and I was able to talk to this man until we landed in Sacramento. He followed me off the airplane.

The pastor and his wife who were there to meet me asked, "Who was that?"

I said, "You didn't recognize that famous musician? He was in disguise."

The pastor's wife said, "It worked. I didn't know him, either."

Chapter 4

The Finishing Touch

Now come with me to Exodus 40. Chapter 40 describes the finishing of the tabernacle, where God was going to come down with His presence and dwell with the people He married in chapter 19. You will notice that there are many references here to Moses' finishing the work.

Verse 16 says: "Thus did Moses; according to all that the Lord commanded him."

Verse 19 says, "...as the Lord had commanded him."

Verse 21 says, "...as the Lord had commanded him."

Verse 33, however, contains the key word: "...So Moses finished the work."

God will crown with glory only assignments you finish. You must finish your assignments!

...So Moses finished the work.

> Then the cloud [the Shekinah, God's visible presence] covered the tent of meeting, and the glory of the Lord filled the tabernacle!
>
> And Moses was not able to enter the tent of meeting because the cloud remained upon it, and the glory of the Lord filled the tabernacle.
>
> In all their journeys whenever the cloud was taken up from over the tabernacle, the Israelites went onward;
>
> But if the cloud was not taken up, they did not journey on till the day that it was taken up.

> For throughout all their journeys the
> cloud of the Lord was upon the tabernacle by
> day, and the fire was in it by night, in the sight
> all of the house of Israel.
>
> Exodus 40:34-38

Finished assignments are important today in the Body of Christ. I know hundreds of people who never finish anything they start. Although they start out with zeal, purpose, and vision, they don't complete their task.

They also get attacked. Once you get a divine assignment from God, you become a prime target for Satan, and he launches his arrows toward you.

Stay in God's presence, and His energizing rest will put you over and accomplish everything He has called you to do. Finish your work!

"IT IS FINISHED!"

When Jesus hung on the cross, He said, "It is finished." However, it wasn't His work that was finished, because He is still interceding for us.

When Jesus said, "It is finished," He was the crowning work of all God's creation. What was finished was His part in closing the old covenant, establishing the new, and building the Church. The first chapter of Hebrews says that God looked upon Jesus and said, "Here, come sit beside Me. I call You God today, and I give You the scepter of righteousness, because You have finished Your assignment, and You are crowned with glory."

The apostle Paul told Timothy, "...I have finished the race...henceforth, there is laid up for me the [victor's] crown of righteousness..." (2 Timothy 4:7,8). God only crowns with glory finished assignments that were done according to His pattern. If you try to complete your assignment any other way, your efforts will not receive the crowning of glory that God desires for you.

Whatever position you're in right now — whether you're in the ministry of helps, between assignments, or having difficulty finishing up — did you know that finishing up is a lot harder than starting out?

If you've ever built a house, you know it's that last month and a half that takes so long — because it's the finishing up.

So Moses finished the tabernacle, his great assignment by which the presence of God came into live intimacy with His people. And the work was crowned with glory. Moses died when he was 120 years old.

TRACING THE PRESENCE OF GOD

Come with me now to the Book of Joshua before we get into the New Testament, and let's trace the manifestation of the presence of God.

The young man Joshua had stayed on his face on the floor of Moses' tent — the tent of God's presence — and he had been trained by Moses.

In Joshua 3:5, Joshua told the people almost exactly the same thing that Moses had told them. Moses told the people to sanctify themselves at the mount of God when God was going to marry them.

Now they were going into Canaan, and Joshua said to the people, "...Sanctify yourselves [that is, separate yourselves for special holy purpose], for tomorrow the Lord will do wonders among you" (Joshua 3:5).

The presence of Almighty God went before the children of Israel through the waters of the Jordan. Joshua wanted the people to be sanctified as they stood in the presence of God and saw the completion of what Moses had started in glory. This task was finished in glory when the children of Israel went into the Promised Land.

In chapter 5, they took the tabernacle to Gilgal, which means "the rolling away of sin." That was where all the males of the new generation were circumcised, which represented the rolling away of sin, the reproach of Egypt.

JOSHUA'S EPIPHANY

Then Joshua had an epiphany, an encounter with the presence of God like Moses had. Verses 13 and 14 tell us:

> When Joshua was by Jericho, he looked up, and behold, a Man stood near him with His drawn sword in His hand. And Joshua went to Him, and said to Him, Are you for us, or for our adversaries?
>
> And He said, No [neither]; but as prince of the Lord's host am I now come....

I believe this was a preincarnate visitation of Jesus Christ, the Second Person of the Trinity!

> ...And Joshua fell on his face to the earth, and worshiped, and said to Him, What says my Lord to His servant?
>
> And the Prince of the Lord's host said to Joshua, "Loose your shoes from off your feet; for the place where you stand is holy. And Joshua did so.
>
> Joshua 5:14,15

The Jews' first battle was the battle of Jericho. As we trace the presence of God, we see that as long as the Jews kept obeying God's pattern, His presence remained with them.

Once the children of Israel arrived in the Promised Land, however, the cloud, the pillar of fire, and the manna were no longer present, because now the people were eating the corn and drinking the wine of Canaan.

FIGHT FOR YOUR INHERITANCE

At some point, the Jews moved the tabernacle from Gilgal to Shiloh. Joshua 18:1 says, "And the whole congregation of the Israelites assembled at Shiloh, and set up the tent of meeting there...." The tent of meeting was Moses' tabernacle.

...and the land was subdued before them.

And there remained among the Israelites seven tribes, to whom their inheritance had not yet been divided.

Joshua asked the Israelites, How long will you be slack to go in and possess the land, which the Lord God of your fathers has given you?

Joshua 18:1-3

In God's presence is your inheritance. That's where you'll find it. And I challenge you: Don't be like the children of Israel. They had a wilderness mentality, because God had taken care of everything for them for 40 years. They'd also had a few battles, but more than half of the tribes never entered in to claim their inheritance.

This percentage is much higher in the Body of Christ today. The percentage of people who have put on their warring clothes and gone into the camp of the enemy to take their inheritance is small, compared to the whole Body of Christ.

Never have I seen more complacent people — people who are content to sit there, fat, dumb, and happy, and let the world go to hell in a handbasket!

But God is getting ready to shake us. He is getting ready to come to us with His fire, His might, and His power and say, "Don't sit here and not take your inheritance."

You need your inheritance! You need your family born again, your land sanctified, and the money that is rightfully yours.

Remember, there is no lack in the presence of God. There is no illness in the presence of God. There is no depression in the presence of God. You can't be in God's presence and keep a sad countenance. You can't be in God's presence and have all kinds of problems plaguing you. In God's presence is fullness of joy forevermore.

Rise up today in the face of every adversity and every adversary, and walk into His presence!

"OFFENSES WILL COME"

In Luke 17:1, Jesus told His disciples, "...Temptations [that is, snares, traps set to entice to sin] are sure to come; but woe to him by or through whom they come!" That's a promise. Jesus knew us, and He added in verse 2, "It would be more profitable for him if a millstone were hung around his neck and he were hurled into the sea, than that he should cause to sin or be a snare to one of these little ones [lowly in rank or influence]."

Peter and the other disciples were listening, and Peter asked, "My God, how often are we supposed to forgive someone?" He had a hard time forgiving once!

When Jesus got through with him, Peter remarked, "Lord, increase our faith." You cannot afford offenses. It is the snare — the bait of the trap — whereby Satan pulls you into the pit of despair and despondency. "Snare" or *skandalon* is the word used in the Greek text.

Dare to be different! Never pick up an offense.

Let that bait lie there. It will drive the person trying to offend you nuts. Say, "I won't pick it up, so go suck on a lemon somewhere else; not in my presence, because I'm not going to do it!"

You must make that decision, because not everyone is going to love you. A lot of people think you're strange, don't they? It's okay. You must simply get to the point in serving God where you don't give a rip. You've made the decision to go on doing what God has called you to do, and you're going to finish your assignment according to the pattern He has laid out. He's the one who will crown your works with glory.

MAD AT A CORPSE

Don't walk through this life holding onto an offense. In prayer lines I've encountered people who have held offenses, and they're still mad at someone who has been dead for 40 years! I lay hands on them first to get their sanity back, and then I wonder how they could stay mad at a corpse for 40 years. I can't understand that. It's beyond my reasoning.

You must die to the flesh until you are dead to what people think about you; until you don't care. Then you won't pick up an offense.

The moment you pick up an offense, your anointing stops — everything stops — because an offense in plain, everyday language is unforgiveness or hurt feelings. You must walk through life without taking offense.

You must "walk on eggs" around some people. I don't like to be around people like that. I want to tell them, "Either get a good attitude, or go away!"

JOHN THE BAPTIST TAKES OFFENSE

One of the greatest stories we have in the Word

of God concerns the time when John the Baptist was thrown in jail for being a dynamic preacher.

His feelings got hurt because he was sitting in jail while Jesus was getting his crowds and performing miracles. John thought, "If He's the Son of God, why isn't He here, delivering me from this jail? He's getting my mailing list. He's getting my television audience. He's getting my crowds — and my disciples."

John's disciples came to see him one day. These men had been his followers, and he asked them, "Why don't you go ask Jesus if He really is the Son of God? Are people getting healed? Are the blind getting their sight restored? Go ask Him if He really is the Messiah."

The Word says that John got offended.

John's disciples asked Jesus John's questions, and Jesus replied, "Go back and tell John that the blind see, the deaf hear, and I am preaching the good news of the kingdom." Then Jesus added, "Oh, and by the way — blessed is he who does not get offended."

Poor John was beheaded, but he wasn't offended when he lost his head. His faith in Jesus as the Messiah had been restored.

EVERYONE OUGHT TO LOVE ME

You can't afford offenses in your life. I don't care what people say — I don't care how you interpret the actions of abuse toward you — you can't afford to walk around with offenses, because when you do, everything stops. You're no longer in God's presence when you are offended.

We've all been offended. I used to think everyone ought to love me because I'm a nice little old lady. When they didn't, I'd sit on the floor and cry, "God, did You hear what they said? Did You see what they wrote about me?"

Our congregation in Tucson started as a Bible study, but when we reached about 500, we started calling it a church. One of the first things that happened afterwards was, I was interviewed by a young woman from a local radio station. It was a Baptist station, and they fired the girl for interviewing a woman pastor.

The next week they called upon their theologian, the big gun in exposing error, to tell their listeners why women can't pastor. I was so embarrassed, and I was hurt for the young woman who had lost her job. I remember sitting on the floor, crying, "God, I've been listening to what the theologian said about me." He wasn't calling my name, but he was talking abut woman pastors, and I was the only one in our city.

God said, "It's okay. I'll take care of him." The man died and went home to glory. But, boy, did he get a surprise in heaven when God said, "She's okay." You'd better watch out when you begin to touch God's anointed. God is in charge!

Put your hand on your heart and say this prayer with me:

PRAYER

Father, I'm greedy for Your presence. Show me more of You. I long to stay in the tent of Your presence. Fill me with your presence so I can minister the true living water to those around me.

God, I promise I will not pick up offenses. Forgive me now if I'm holding anything in my life against anyone, dead or alive. I release it right now. I forgive them, I set them free, and I'm free in Jesus' Name.

And Holy Spirit, work on me. Work on my emotions. Don't let me be fragile in areas Satan could take my feelings and use them against me. Help me grow up. Perfect me. I thank You, Jesus, for Your presence. Amen.

CHAPTER 5

A CALL TO HOLINESS

We've got to grow up, folks! We've got to do things right, because we don't have enough time left to keep making mistakes. We've got to get moving in doing what God wants us to do.

As we've seen, God's presence will not dwell with sin. That's why there is a call to holiness in the Church today that we haven't heard for a long time. It's time for us to clean up our lives.

Don't watch junk on television. Don't let filthy novels and other materials come into your house. Things that are in front of your eyes are things you meditate on, and soon they drop down into your heart, and you become those things!

There has never been so much trash in the world as there is today — and God is calling us to holiness. We need to hold to a high standard in the Church. We need to be a holy people, a sanctified people who are walking in God's presence.

If we aren't a holy people, we will experience the judgment arm of Christ as well as the mercy arm of Christ. One of the signs of the end times is, we will see some Ananiases and Sapphiras.

Ananias came to the early service and lied and died. Sapphira came to the second service and lied and fried. Both were carried out of the church, dead.

You cannot lie to the Holy Spirit and get away with it when the presence of God is present in that dimension of power in the Church. That's what we are coming to again. I want a church like that, so when people come in the front door, they know they can't be hypocritical; they can't do anything sinful.

If you're a sinner, come in and get saved. God is not going to knock you down. However, He is requiring a lot more from those of us who are mature in the faith and know better. He wants us to live clean lives before Him.

SIN INVADES THE CAMP

The ark of the covenant accompanied the children of Israel through all their journeys, including their conquest of the land of Canaan.

Now we come to one of the saddest pictures in history. In First Samuel, we get a glimpse of what really happens when sin literally invades the camp.

Chapter 1 tells the story of Hannah, the barren wife who cried and prayed for God to give her a child. When her son Samuel was born, she gave him to God, and he lived in the tabernacle where the prophet Eli was the priest. Eli had two wicked sons, Hophni and Phinehas, who are described in First Samuel 2:12 as "base and worthless."

Everyone thinks I make this stuff up, but it is in the Bible. I see the Bible like a videotape, and it is the most exciting book! Did you know the Bible is a racy book if you know how to read it? You'll learn everything you want to know in the Bible. Simply remove the blinders off your eyes.

Samuel grew up in the tabernacle, and one night the lad heard the voice of God. First Samuel 3:1 records, "Now the boy Samuel ministered to the Lord before Eli. The word of the Lord was rare and precious in those days; there was no frequent or widely spread vision." It was because there was so much sin in the camp!

A PRIEST'S SONS GONE BAD

Chapter 2 tells us about Eli's wicked sons. These two young men committed adultery on the very steps of the tabernacle! They also stole from the offerings.

When the people would bring their meat offerings, Eli's sons would take big meat hooks, run them through the meat, and take the fat, which was God's portion, a portion that was to be burned and rise as smoke before God.

Eli's sons were greedy for money and sex, but God will not put up with the junk that was going on in the tabernacle. No wonder the Word of God was rare, and there was no widespread vision. These greedy guys were ruining the offerings.

The Bible says that the people had no regard for the offerings, because these wicked priests were taking the fat that was to be smoke that would go up before God.

God sent a nameless prophet to Eli, and he warned sternly, "If you don't get your house in order, you know you are going to die." But Eli did nothing to restrain his sons.

The children of Israel went out to battle against the Philistines in chapter 4, but they lost the battle. At first, 4,000 Jews were killed, and 30,000 more were killed in the next battle.

The Jews remembered the victories they'd had around Jericho and the little villages in Canaan, and they knew that God's presence had been the key in those victories. So they said, "Let's go get the ark of the covenant and bring it with us into battle, and we'll whip these Philistines."

They returned to Shiloh and got the ark of the covenant. Those ungodly priests Hophni and Phinehas accompanied the ark into the battle. As they came to the front lines with the ark, the Israelites started screaming, hollering, clapping, singing, and dancing, because here came the ark!

WHEN GOD ISN'T IN THE "BOX"

When the Philistines heard this, it scared them. They said, "Oh my, they're bringing their God-in-the-box to the battle, and we'll lose." It was a trauma for the Philistines. But what the Philistines didn't know was there was sin in the Jews' camp — and God wasn't in the box anymore!

I've been in churches where God was a million miles away, yet the people went through the same old same old motions, even though nothing happened.

The children of Israel screamed, hollered, and said, "We'll win! We'll win!" But God wasn't there. He's not in the noise, He's not deaf, and He's not nervous, either. He doesn't mind loud noises.

The Philistines were traumatized, but when the armies went into battle the next day, the Israelites lost, and 30,000 Israelites were killed in "a very great slaughter" (verse 10).

A little guy went running back to the tabernacle at Shiloh and saw Eli, the 98-year-old high priest, sitting out in front on a little stool.

The messenger threw himself on the ground in front of Eli and gasped, "A terrible thing has happened! We lost the battle today. The Philistines have won, your two sons are dead — and the worst thing of all is, they stole the ark of the covenant!"

As Eli listened to this, he was crushed because his sons were dead. But the Word says his heart was broken because the ark of the covenant was stolen, and it was stolen by a heathen tribe called the Philistines, and Eli died. The Philistines worshipped the god Dagon, who was half fish and half man — he was a merman — and the Philistines had a temple that was dedicated to him.

HEATHENS AND THE PRESENCE OF GOD

The Philistines didn't know what to do with the ark, because heathens don't know what to do with the presence of God. I have learned something exciting from this story. Did you know that God will manifest Himself among heathens or backslidden Christians when He wants to? He manifested Himself to these Philistines.

In the temple of Dagon there was no pulpit, but they placed their idols up on pedestals. Dagon, the fish god, was in the center. Since the Philistines didn't know what to do with the God-in-the-box, they took the ark inside and set it down beside Dagon.

God looked over and said, "I don't like that fish man!" When the Philistines entered the temple the next morning, Dagon was knocked off his perch, and that had never happened before. They picked him up, dusted him off, put him back on his pedestal, and left.

When they returned the next day, their god was not only knocked off his perch; some of his body parts had been broken off! They glued him back together, put him back on his pedestal, and thought correctly, "We don't think the Jewish God-in-the-box wants to be in here with Dagon!"

Because they didn't know what to do with the God-in-the-box, they sent Him on a tour of three Philistine cities.

"SEND IT BACK!"

Everywhere the ark went, the people got painful tumors and an infestation of mice. The *King James Version* uses the word, "emerods," but *The Amplified Bible* says "tumors," and I like that better. Because tumors and mice appeared wherever the ark went, I'm sure the women hated to see that box coming down the road! They didn't want it in their land, "for there was a deadly panic throughout all the city" (1 Samuel 5:11).

Finally, in First Samuel 6, the Philistines had had enough and decided, "Let's send it back!" This heathen tribe had kept the ark for seven months, and it had brought them nothing but trouble. They chose two milk cows, built a cart, hitched the cows to it, and sent the ark back to Israel with gold guilt offerings in it, the Philistine leaders following at a very discreet distance.

The ark symbolized the presence of God.

And they put the ark of the Lord on the cart, and the box with the mice of gold, and the images of their tumors.

And the cows went straight toward Beth-shemesh [a little village] along the highway, lowing as they went, and turned not aside to the right or the left, and the Philistine lords followed them as far as the border of Beth-shemesh.

1 Samuel 6:11,12

THE PRESENCE RETURNS AT HARVEST TIME

This next verse, verse 13, is prophetic.

Now the men of Beth-shemesh were reaping their wheat harvest in the valley; and they lifted up their eyes and saw the ark, and rejoiced to see it.

This was a wonderful thing! God's presence came back to Israel, where it belonged — and it came at harvest time.

We are in the time of harvest now, and God is bringing back His presence to the Church. In fact, we can't accomplish this harvest without God's presence coming back to the Church — to live in the

Church — for harvest.

There is always fruit in the presence of God. That's exactly why the presence of God is coming to the Church: for the harvest.

Even the Jews didn't know what to do with the ark. Finally they put it in the house of Abinadab. It remained there for almost 100 years, according to *The Amplified Bible*, through the entire judgeship of Samuel, through the reign of Saul, and way into the reign of King David (1 Samuel 7:2).

A CHURCH WITHOUT GOD

Can you imagine going to church that has been without the presence of God for 100 years? This is an indictment, isn't it, against the priesthood of Israel? The ark remained in that little house for a century, and the Bible doesn't record that anyone ever went to see it or retrieve it. I think Abinadab's sons, Uzzah and Ahio, played on the ark as if it were a piece of furniture! They didn't know any better.

We, too, have raised several generations that have no fear of the Lord. They don't know how to act around the presence of God, yet reverence and awesome godly fear are what keep the presence of God in our midst. When people are irreverent — when they don't care about the presence of God — it grieves the Holy Spirit of God, and His presence lifts.

Death happens when you don't know how to treat the presence of God.

When I was a little girl, my mother and daddy were both ministers, and my mother would never let me turn around in my seat in church. However, when I was 4 years old, we visited Angelus Temple in Los Angeles, and Mother said, "You can turn around now, because Sister McPherson is about to come down the stairs." I got to turn around that day, and it was the first time I ever remember getting to turn around in church.

REVERENCE FOR ALMIGHTY GOD

We weren't allowed to chew gum, and we couldn't take coloring books to church. Although we were little kids, we learned reverence for Almighty God. It was awesome how we were reared.

I see a generation today that doesn't have this reverence for God. However, it's not their fault. Their parents didn't teach them to reverence God, for the presence of God in their midst was not strong enough for the parents to say, "Don't be irreverent."

CHAPTER 6

PREPARING FOR HARVEST TIME

The ark was back! It was back in Israel again! It had stayed in Abinadab's little house for almost 100 years, through all of Samuel's being raised up as an influential prophet, his Bible schools, and all the time Saul was king. Saul's death is recorded in the last chapter of First Samuel.

David had a hunger in his heart for God that brought the glory back to Israel. It takes a man or a woman with a hunger for the presence of God to mobilize and get a group going toward the presence of God.

David often talked about his enemies in the early chapters of the Psalms. In Psalm 41:10-12, he wrote:

> But do You, O Lord, be merciful and gracious to me and raise me up, that I may requite them.
>
> By this I know that You favor and delight in me, because my enemy does not triumph over me.
>
> And as for me, You have upheld me in my integrity, and set me in Your presence for ever.

This is a psalm of praise. I think that when David was a little shepherd boy alone on the hills of Judaea, he penned these beautiful songs when he was in the presence of God.

When David triumphed over Goliath and left his lonely shepherd's job to move to Saul's palace, he was the hero of the whole nation. Eventually, Saul got jealous and became angry with him. Later, there were times when David returned to the wilderness, this time as a hunted man, living in caves and hiding from King Saul's murderous wrath.

Throughout this time, as you will see in the Psalms, David reflected and wrote, "God, I trust in You. You are my fortress. I don't want to live without You. I want to be in Your presence forever." David talked a great deal about the presence of God. David was anointed king of Israel three times. He was anointed first as a boy by the prophet Samuel. Second, he was anointed by his brothers from the Tribe of Judah. His third anointing in Hebron made him king over all of Israel at age 30.

Beginning in Second Samuel 5, he said to the prophet Nathan and a group of people, "Let's go get the ark of the covenant!"

DAVID PREPARES FOR THE PRESENCE OF GOD

We're also going to look at this story in First Chronicles. There is a key phrase in First Chronicles 15:1: "David...prepared a place for the ark of God...."

The ark had not been used in public worship for 100 years, so David knew nothing about the ark or the presence of God in public worship. He had always known the presence of God privately. Now he hungered to have the whole nation know the presence of God, so he called a large group together and announced, "We're going to go get the ark of God, and we're going to make a place for it here in Jerusalem."

David constructed a little tent for the ark on Mount Zion, near the site of his palace. The little tent covering the ark was not spectacular; nevertheless, David was preparing the people and the place.

Pastors, you must prepare a place for the presence of God, first in yourself, and then in your people. Then God will come in, because God wants to come in more than you want Him to. Oh, when the presence of God comes into the tent of His presence!

After David announced, "We're going to go get the ark of the covenant," he asked, "How did they get the ark to the house of Abinadab?"

The people told him, "The Philistines sent it back on a cart."

David said, "That sounds good to me!"

PROJECTS TAKE TWO GENERATIONS

It takes two generations to complete any major project of God, but David didn't have a predecessor to tell him how to get the presence of God or how to transport the ark. And because he didn't know the details, a man named Uzzah died.

They went to get the ark; they put it on a new cart; and they started down the hill toward Nacon's threshing floor. The oxen stumbled on the rutted road, the ark started rocking back and forth, and Uzzah reached his hand out and touched the ark to steady it.

The ark had been in his father's house for 100 years, and Uzzah had gotten too familiar with the presence of God. Thus, he violated an important principle. When he touched the ark, he touched the presence of God — and he died on the spot!

What had been a time of joy, singing, and rejoicing turned into a time of mourning. The Bible says that David got offended at God. He said, "Dear God, see my heart. Don't You know I was trying to get Your presence back to Jerusalem? Why did You take this young man's life? Why did You make a fool out of me? Dear God, what have I done? I'm only trying to get Your presence." But there is order in everything God does.

David returned home, and the people gingerly

took the ark of the covenant and set it in a little house at Nacon's threshing floor. It was the house of Obed-edom, who lived at the threshing floor. History tells us he was a farmer.

RICH IN ONLY 90 DAYS!

I can imagine they took a window out of his house to slide the ark inside. They moved the cart over to the house very gently, three or four men got on one end of the ark, and they slid it into the house of Obed-edom. No one wanted to touch it now. Even David was afraid of the Lord that day, according to Second Samuel 6:9.

Are you ready for this? The ark stayed in that farmer's house for 90 days. And in those 90 days, he got so rich from the presence of God, he left the farm, joined the choir in Jerusalem, and became a gate-keeper and a singer! He got that rich from the presence of God in only 90 days!

In the presence of God there is no lack.

In the presence of God there are riches for every project.

In the presence of God is everything you'll ever need.

Obed-edom didn't know he was going to be blessed like that. He was just standing there fat, dumb, and happy, and all of a sudden here came that box sliding through the window right into his living room, and it was the presence of God!

Obed-edom got rich and blessed. In fact, the Bible says that everything he had got blessed. His kids got blessed, his cattle got blessed, his farm got blessed — and in 90 days he was so rich, he left the farm and moved to the city! I think that's an awesome story!

DAVID LEARNED HIS LESSON

Meanwhile, David went back home and began to pray. All this is recorded in Second Samuel 5.

In First Chronicles 13, we find the same story, with a little different slant on it. Verses 13 and 14 relate:

> So David did not bring the ark home to the city of David, but carried it aside into the house of Obed-edom the Gittite [a Levitical porter, born in Gathrimmon].

> And the ark of God remained with the family of Obed-edom in his house three months. And the Lord blessed the house of Obed-edom, and all that he had.

Isn't that wonderful? The beginning of chapter 15 will also bless you. David had built many houses for himself, but notice verse 1: "David made him houses in the city of David, and he prepared a place for the ark of God, and pitched a tent for it."

By now David had read the book Moses wrote, and he said, "None should carry the ark of God but the Levites; for the Lord chose them to carry the ark of God and to minister to Him for ever" (verse 2).

We see David's preparations again in verse 3: "And David assembled all Israel at Jerusalem, to bring up the ark of the Lord to its place, which he had prepared for it."

A TIME FOR SANCTIFYING

A similar season of preparation is what we're in right now. It's a season of repenting. We're getting ready — we're getting the junk out of our lives — so we can have the presence of God. We are preparing a place for the presence of God.

David gathered all the Levites, and he called for

Zadok and Abiathar, the priests, as he was getting everyone ready. In verse 12, he told them, "You are the heads of the fathers' houses of the Levites; sanctify yourselves, both you and your brethren, that you may bring up the ark of the Lord, the God of Israel, to the place that I have prepared for it." Three times the Bible says David prepared for it.

You will never have the presence of God until you sanctify yourselves.

David explained in verse 2 (my paraphrase), "Because we didn't do it right the first time — the way God directed — He broke out on us. The Levites should have carried the ark all the time."

Watch this, musicians! This is an awesome lesson about the tabernacle of David. The Old Testament prophet Amos told us that the tabernacle of David would be restored. Then James, the pastor in Jerusalem, told us in Acts 15 in the New Testament that the tabernacle of David was being restored to the Church.

It's important that you see this, because I'll show you things about this tabernacle that are coming to the Church.

In verse 16, "David told the chief Levites to appoint their brethren the singers with instruments of music, harps, lyres and cymbals, to play loudly and lift up their voices with joy." Then these people were named, and Obed-edom was one of those listed in verse 18. I told you he joined the choir!

THE END OF SACRIFICES

Now I want to contrast the difference between sacrifices held at the tabernacle of Moses and the end of those sacrifices when the ark was moved to the tent in Jerusalem.

There were always bloody sacrifices at the tabernacle of Moses — blood, blood, blood all the time. The people brought every kind of animal possible to sacrifice. But there were never any blood sacrifices at the tabernacle after the day they moved the ark to Mount Zion.

As the people made their way up to Mount Zion that day, they sacrificed a bull every six paces. They marched through the blood with the presence of God, and then they sang and marched another few steps. It took them all day to pass through that bloody trail, taking the ark from the house of Obed-edom to the tent that David had prepared for it.

After they offered the final blood sacrifices, there were never any more blood sacrifices offered at David's tabernacle. Why? Because the proper sacrifice was now the fruit of their lips as they gave the sacrifice of praise to Almighty God!

David appointed the singers. They were dressed in white linen ephods when they went to get the ark. They brought it back with a great deal of sanctification and trepidation.

THE HIGH PRIEST'S PREPARATION

In the past, the High Priest had to sanctify himself carefully before he entered into the tabernacle once a year to make atonement for the children of Israel. He spent months getting ready to go into the presence of God.

If there was any sin in his life, he died there in the presence of God. The hem of his robe was trimmed with bells and cymbals, and a rope was tied around his ankle. If those bells stopped ringing while he was sprinkling the blood on the mercy seat in the tabernacle, they would pull his body out of the tabernacle by that rope.

Jesus is going to sit on the throne of David, not

the throne of Solomon. Why? Because David had a revelation of grace. When he brought the ark back to Jerusalem, he put it in that little tent — but a veil was no longer placed over the doorway.

When the ark was in Moses' tabernacle, a veil of skins covered the entrance, and no one went behind that veil except the High Priest once a year, or when the High Priest would wrap the ark in sealskin before moving it to the next place. It was carried on the shoulders of men from the tribe of Kohath, the porters.

A WORD FROM THE LORD

This reminds me of a trip I made to Kenya several years ago to hold meetings in two cities. I was exhausted after ministering, and some friends and I took a day off to drive through the countryside. I was trying to relax, watching zebras, monkeys, and other animals, and I was having a wonderful time.

Suddenly, the Spirit of the Lord invaded that station wagon, and I began to weep. He began to talk to me. The other women also began to weep and pray. Finally my friend Valerie punched me on the shoulder and asked, "What is the Spirit saying?"

This was right after we had come through the scandals of certain television ministries in the United States. The Lord said, "I am going to bring the glory back to the Church on the shoulders of sanctified leaders and on the wings of praise and worship."

He burned these words into my heart, and I have never forgotten them. That's why I get so excited when I teach on this subject.

When God says, "I am going to bring the glory back," He is going to bring back His manifested presence. *Kabod*, the weightiness of the glory of God, is

His presence coming into our midst.

DAVID'S REVELATION OF GRACE

David had now brought the ark of the covenant to Jerusalem. Because he'd had a revelation of grace, no longer was there a veil over God's presence. While the ark was on Mount Zion, it was in an open tent, and anyone could walk right up to it.

No longer was the presence of God limited to an individual, the High Priest; now it was available to a nation. It was for anyone — for "whosoever will."

Now any Jew could stand in front of David's tabernacle with his hands in the air, listening to the trumpeters and the other musicians who were playing harps and lyres, and he could worship God with a "naked face" — with nothing between him and the presence of God. That's pure grace!

WHEN THE GLORY OF GOD ROLLED IN

Once I was preaching about the ark in Dothan, Alabama. They'd had a miniature ark built. It was a Saturday night, and the building was full.

They have a great drama team in that church, and when I saw smoke rolling in under the doors, I thought the young people were playing with a smoke machine out in the lobby. I thought, "Those dumb kids!" but I didn't say anything.

As the smoke reached each aisle, the people "disappeared" from sight! They were on the floor, they were praying, or they were being really quiet. I still didn't know what was happening, because I hadn't seen the glory in that dimension in probably 35 years.

Then it began to roll toward the front of the church. As it got to each row, the people fell off the seats. Pastor Kennan Batchelor is nearly 7 feet tall, and he was stretched out on the floor like he was dead.

The glory of God was in that place! We couldn't move, it was so weighty in there. Although we could all see the glory, we couldn't see through it.

We were in that glory for several hours. The young woman who was traveling with me was still shaken when we returned to the hotel. She'd never been in a service like that. I said, "Now, Sugar, let me teach you something. When God manifests His glory like this, there will always be fruit as a result."

When we returned to church the next morning, the glory of God was still in the building. Although it was not present in the same dimension, it was still powerful. As I ministered, there was weeping. I kept waiting, because I knew there would be fruit.

FRUIT FOLLOWS MANIFESTATION

That night, a man stood up and said, "Pastor, can I testify?"

The pastor said, "Sure, come on up."

The man was a construction foreman. He said, "Last night I was in here when that wave of glory came in. I've never been in anything like it in my life. I couldn't move. I wept until I felt like great roots had been pulled up out of me. I just wept in the presence of God."

"My wife came over this morning. Our divorce was to be final Thursday. The glory of God did the same thing to her last night. We spent all afternoon together, and we are reconciled."

Glory always bears fruit, because flesh has to die in the presence of God. I have seen this firsthand many times.

DAVID'S CELEBRATION

David was so excited! He had organized the bringing back of the ark, and he danced himself happy as they brought it back.

First Chronicles 16:1-4 says:

So they brought the ark of God, and set it in the midst of the tent which David had pitched for it; and they offered burnt offerings and peace offerings before God.

And when David had finished offering the burnt offerings and the peace offerings, he blessed the people in the name of the Lord.

And he distributed to every one of Israel, both man and woman, to every one a loaf of bread, a portion of meat, and a cake of raisins [that's chocolate chip cookies].

He appointed Levites to minister before the ark of the Lord, and to celebrate (by calling to mind), thanking and praising the Lord, the God of Israel.

This is the only example in history of a monarch giving everyone in his nation bread and wine.

David went home after this picnic. His first wife, Michal, had seen him dancing in the procession, "...leaping as in sport, and she despised him in her heart" (1 Chronicles 15:29). Michal, the youngest daughter of King Saul, was David's prize for killing Goliath.

Michal was once madly in love with David. He was everyone's hero, because he was an awesome young man. However, Saul got so angry at David, he separated David and Michal, and he gave her to a man whose name was Phalti.

When David became king, he said, "There is one more thing I want." This was years and years later, and he had several other wives, but he said, "I want my first wife back. I want Michal back."

Saul's son Ishbosheth agreed to his request and sent for Michal, who was now married to Phalti. They knocked on the door and announced, "David wants you to come back. You're his wife. He's never given you a legal divorce; that was your father's doing."

DAVID REGAINS HIS FIRST WIFE

Michal said, "I don't want to go. I've been married to Phalti for years, and I'm in love with him. David can go and suck a lemon for all I care. I don't want to get involved with him again!"

The messengers said, "You don't have a choice."

As Michal walked toward the palace, angry and rebellious, Phalti followed like a little dog, weeping. You'll find this story in the Word if you think I'm making it up. See Second Samuel 3. Finally, David's ally Abner stomped his foot and ordered, "Go home, Phalti!" — and Phalti went home without Michal.

When Michal got to the palace, she was mad as a wet hen. She hated it, and she didn't want a thing to do with David. A few years later, as Michal stood there, she watched the parade coming up the hill toward the palace.

She also saw David in his priestly ephod, leaping, dancing, rejoicing, and having a wonderful time. Everyone was enjoying the presence of God.

DAVID SHARES HIS HEART

After King David gave everyone in his kingdom cakes, meat, and wine, he went home and said, "Oh, Michal, did you see that party? I can't tell you how my heart feels tonight!

"Look over here, Michal. Do you see the little ark? That symbolizes God's presence, and now we have it again! It's been gone 100 years, but now everyone in Israel can come and worship God, standing before Him with naked faces.

"Here, raise the window. Listen to that music. Did you know I've ordered the musicians to play 24 hours a day? Before, there was a curtain over the ark. Now this worship music forms the veil."

That's why music is so important in this move of God. Musicians, I'll tell you by the Spirit of God, there are notes to be sung and songs to be written that have not yet come into your minds.

There are places in the realm of God's music that He's going to take this generation that you've never been to before. The most awesome thing is that this music, the wings of praise and worship, will be the veil that protects us by grace and leads us into the awesome presence of God.

MICHAL ISN'T IMPRESSED

Praise and worship were going on 24 hours a day at David's tabernacle on Zion. As we know, David was always passionate about music.

David said, "Oh, Michal, listen to that music! You can go and stand in front of the very presence of God anytime, and nothing will happen to you, because the musicians are offering the sacrifice of praise up to God with the fruit of their lips.

Michal replied, "David, I think that's stupid! I'm a king's daughter — a princess — and we didn't go to that church. It's a crazy church. You guys clap and dance. You read words off the wall instead of out of a hymnal. You don't even have regular pews; you sit on chairs. And you stand the whole time you sing. I hate that church of yours, David!"

She added, "And you dance. I saw you coming down the road today. You were dancing that

Charismatic two-step, and your ephod was flopping open. Every handmaiden saw your BVDs. You were vile!

"I'm so embarrassed and humiliated, I can't even go to the grocery store. I can just see *The National Enquirer* headline: 'King Flashes Handmaidens.' I can never go out in public again, because I'm so humiliated by your worship."

David sat in his lounge chair sipping a soft drink and let her rave on. I love what he said in the *King James Version* (my paraphrase): "You ain't seen nothin' yet, baby! Today is only the first day of the revival. We've got the presence of God back, and I'm going to get even more 'vile,' hallelujah! Thank You, Jesus! I'm going to let it rip."

The word "vile" means "unrestrained." David said, "I'm going to get even wilder in my praise to God. We haven't had God living with us for 100 years. We haven't even known how to act in the presence of God. It's been 100 years, Michal!"

DON'T RECEIVE MICHAL'S EPITAPH

The Word writes Michal's epitaph right here. It says, "And Michal the daughter of Saul had no child to the day of her death" (2 Samuel 6:23).

If you touch this move of God with your mouth, you will not have any intimacy with the King of Kings, and you will be barren until the day you die.

History tells us that David never slept with Michal after her outburst that day; there was never any more intimacy between them.

I'm warning you: If you ever touch this move of God with your mouth in judgment, criticism, or harshness, you will be barren until the day you die. There will be no fruit in your life, because God will not bless a critical spirit.

Did you know you can get offended over the way other people worship God? You can come to church and get totally offended over things that are going on; and when you do, barrenness is all that will ever come into your life.

There was never any music in the Mosaic tabernacle. The old order of Zadok was left three and a half miles away on Mount Gibeon with the old tent of Moses. There was nothing left in the old tent except the old furniture, because the ark of the covenant was no longer there.

They moved it from Shiloh to Gibeon, which was three and a half miles from Zion. The old tent of Moses was made in the wilderness, but the presence of God had not been in it since the days of Eli. Nevertheless, the Jews went on with their sacrifices, burnt offerings, and so forth.

There was no music in that tabernacle; at least none that we can find any record of. We know that Moses, Miriam, and others sang, but it wasn't in the tabernacle. In my studies of the Mosaic tabernacle, it seems that no music was ever performed in it.

Chapter 7

David's Dream House

Coming to Second Samuel 7, we find that one day as King David was looking out a palace window, he turned to the prophet Nathan and said (my paraphrase), "Nathan, I tell you, every time I look out the window, I start to weep.

"The most wonderful thing you can imagine is our having the presence of God, but it really bothers me that the ark is still housed in that little tent. It's been there for several years, and the tent is wearing out.

"I've decided to build God a house that will be so spectacular, it will be one of the seven wonders of the world! Why should I live in this palace of cedar, gold, and other beautiful things when God lives in that little tent? I'm going to build God a house worthy of His presence!"

Do you see David's heart, pastors? He was always preparing a place for the presence of God — always. He didn't get too high, too low, or too discouraged; he was always devoted to this task.

After all, God won't barge in on you. He wants to live with you in the worst way, but you must prepare the place for Him.

I can tell you exactly where the tent of His presence is for me. It's anywhere I am on the road; but when I'm home, I've got a white leather chair in my den, and on the left side of it is a little basket of Bibles, confessions, and prayers that I pray.

When I'm sitting there, the tent of God's presence is all over me! I can sit in that chair and get in God's presence in two seconds, and I don't want to move. It's that weightiness of God's presence. He and I talk about the most awesome, intimate things in that tent of His presence.

As we saw, Joshua stayed on his face in the presence of God in Moses' personal prayer tent, not in the tabernacle. God has charged me to build a tent of His presence for this generation, because every major move of God takes two generations to accomplish: Moses and Joshua; David and Solomon; Peter, James, and John, and then the major writers of the New Testament, Paul, Timothy, and Luke.

Although I am supposed to build a prayer tent, I can't force you into my tent; I must invite you to come inside. Therefore, I invite you to come into the tent of God's presence!

So David said in Second Samuel 7:2, "Oh, Nathan, we've got to build God a house!"

And Nathan replied, "That's a wonderful idea, David. I believe we ought to treat God with respect." However, that night God talked to Nathan. He said, "Nathan, I didn't ask David to build Me a house."

NOT A GOD IDEA

God can tear up all our plans in about a minute and a half. We get all these great, big wonderful plans. I remember a time I was going to feed the hungry. It was a good idea, but it wasn't a God idea, and I got into a big mess. Now I give money to those who are called to feed the hungry. I've learned that a need is not a call.

Now let me show you some things in verses 4 through 13. There are seven parts to this.

That night, the word of the Lord came to Nathan, saying,

Go and tell My servant David, Thus says the Lord: Shall you build Me a house in which to dwell?

For I have not dwelt in a house since I brought the Israelites out of Egypt to this day, but have moved about with a tent for My dwelling.

Here, the Lord was referring to the Mosaic tabernacle and the Davidic tabernacle.

In all places where I have moved with all the Israelites, did I speak a word to any from the tribes of Israel whom I commanded to be shepherd of My people Israel, asking, Why do you not build Me a house of cedar?

So now say this to My servant David, Thus says the Lord of hosts, I took you from the pasture [here is where the Davidic covenant starts], from following the sheep, to be prince over My people Israel.

I was with you wherever you went, and have cut off all your enemies from before you, and I will make you a great name, like [that] of the great of the earth.

And I will appoint a place for My people Israel, and will plant them, that they may dwell in a place of their own, and be moved no more; and wicked men shall afflict them no more as formerly,

And as from the time that I appointed judges over My people Israel; I will cause you to rest from all your enemies. Also the Lord declares to you that He will make for you a house.

And when your days are fulfilled, and you sleep with your fathers, I will set up after you your offspring who shall be born to you, and I will establish his kingdom.

> He shall build a house for My name [and
> My presence] and I will establish the throne of
> his kingdom for ever.

Verse 12 speaks of Solomon, David's offspring.
God had to pass over David's firstborn son, Amnon,
who was the primogenitor, because of Amnon's own
sin. David's younger son Solomon was the one God
chose to build the Temple.

A MESSIANIC PROMISE

Verse 13 is a Messianic promise that speaks
about Jesus' building a house for God's Name and
His presence. In turn, God promises to establish His
throne — the throne of His kingdom — forever.

Then, in verses 14-16 God resumes speaking of
Solomon:

> I will be his Father, and he shall be My
> son. When he commits iniquity, I will chasten
> him with the rod of men, and with the stripes
> of the sons of men;

> But My mercy and loving-kindness shall
> not depart from him, as I took [them] from
> Saul, whom I took away before you.

> And your house and your kingdom shall
> be made sure for ever before you; your throne
> shall be established for ever.

JACOB'S INHERITANCE

Now let's take a quick trip back to Genesis 49.
This chapter contains the prophecies and the inheri-
tances Jacob gave to his sons. When he lay dying, he
called them to his bedside. As each put his hand
under Jacob's thigh, he received Jacob's blessing.

The primogenitor, Jacob's firstborn son by Leah,
was Reuben. Reuben should have been the one who
received all the inheritance. Jacob told him, "Reuben,

put your hand under my thigh, because I'm going to bless you, but you cannot receive the primogenitor's portion, because you committed fornication and adultery with my concubine Bilhah (Genesis 35:22). When you violated your father's bed, it disqualified you from being the patriarch of the family and getting the double portion." Reuben got a lesser portion, and he was dismissed.

Next, Jacob called Simeon and Levi. He said, "You boys should have gotten the primogenitor's inheritance, but you can't, because in vindicating your sister Dinah's rape, you went into a camp and killed all the people there, including the innocent. Thus, you have bloodguiltiness on your hands, and neither of you can become the patriarch of the family or receive the double portion of the inheritance, either."

JACOB NAMES HIS SUCCESSOR

The fourth son was named Judah. Jacob called Judah in and said, "Judah, your brothers will all praise you. You will be the patriarch of this whole family."

Then Jacob began to prophesy to Judah. He said (my paraphrase), "You will be like a lion that goes up high in the mountains, and comes down again. The staff of rulership will not depart from between your feet until Shiloh [or Messiah] comes. He will bind His foal to the vine and his donkey's colt to the choice vine."

The reference to a lion points to Jesus the Messiah, because He is called "the lion of the tribe of Judah." Jacob's reference to a vine means that Jesus was coming to the house of Israel, the vine.

You must get this down in your spirit. When it does, it will set you afire. I get blessed by every word in the Book, including genealogies.

WHY TAMAR SEDUCED JUDAH

You may remember the clever seduction of Judah by Tamar. David comes from this lineage.

I tell you, the Bible is a racy book! Tamar, the scorned young widow; Rahab, the harlot; and Bathsheba, Solomon's beautiful mother, were women we might not respect, yet they were among the ancestors of Jesus!

This is what happened to Tamar. Judah's first son, Er, the primogenitor, died before he and Tamar could have a child, so the young widow was given to the second son, Onan, according to the Jewish marriage law which was followed then.

She was supposed to have a son raised under Er's name so he could get the inheritance. Widows had no standing in Israel at that time. Onan wanted to have sex with her, all right, but he didn't want her to get pregnant, because he didn't want her child to get the inheritance!

So Onan practiced a form of birth control that displeased God, and God killed him. By then Tamar was probably known as "the black widow." Judah had one remaining son, Shelah, but he was too young to be married.

Judah told Tamar, "I'll give Shelah to you when he's old enough," but he didn't have any intention of doing that, and he sent her back home.

TAMAR'S REVENGE

Tamar went home young, poor, and broken-hearted, realizing that Judah was never going to give her to Shelah. She desperately wanted a baby. Her solution was to dress like a prostitute from a heathen temple and accost her father-in-law.

To do that, Tamar wore that era's equivalent of a

skimpy top, short black skirt, red high heels, and tons of makeup. She went swinging down the street chewing bubble gum and twisting her purse.

She also wore a veil, so Judah didn't know who she was. He thought she was a temple prostitute, and he willingly went with her when she lured him into a dark little room. I've seen those prostitutes' rooms in heathen temples.

Tamar said, "Put your money down."

Her father-in-law said, "Oh, I didn't bring any money with me. I came to sell my sheep."

She said, "Sorry, buster. No money, no fun. What do you have with you?"

"Well," he said, "I've got my Medicare card, my Social Security Card — what do you want?" She shrewdly talked him out of leaving his belt, his signet ring, and his staff. Staffs like his were engraved with family genealogies.

If he had been hit by a Cadillac when he walked out of there, no one would have known who he was, because Tamar had every bit of his identification!

TAMAR ESCAPES DEATH

That little encounter got Tamar pregnant — with twins! The people wanted to stone her to death for adultery, and Judah was first in line. After all, she was his daughter-in-law, and the honor of his house was at stake — or so he thought.

But she said, "Wait just a minute, Judah. Before you stone me to death, here is the identification of the man who is the father of these children." And Judah probably fainted!

When he came to, he admitted, "She has done more righteously than I." According to the Jewish law covering marriage, he should have given her to his remaining son, Shelah. To make a long story short, Tamar's twins, Perez and Zerah, are also in the lineage of David and Jesus.

As Nathan gave David the Davidic Covenant, he referred to this genealogy, which went all the way back to Genesis. And all of it also pointed forward to the Messiah, Jesus Christ.

David was floored when God said, "I am going to build you a house, David. I didn't ask you to build Me a house for My presence. But because you love Me, I'm going to let you raise all the money; I'm going to let you draw up all the plans; and I'm going to let you do all the architectural work. I'm going to let you do everything for it. Keep worshipping over here and encouraging the people to come here, too.

Until then, worship at the tabernacle had been conducted by the priests, but now it was a personal act, allowing everyone to enter into the very presence of God.

After all the preparatory work for the Temple was done, David died, and Solomon became king. He had seen how much his father wanted the presence of God — more than his next breath.

So Solomon said, "O God, I want to be that kind of king!" And the first thing he asked God for was wisdom. God granted him great wisdom, and he built the magnificent Temple his father had envisioned.

THE DEDICATION OF THE TEMPLE

Second Chronicles 5 tells us that when the Temple was finished, and they moved all the furnishings into it, the trumpeters played. (I don't understand the full significance of all this yet, but I'm going to.)

They removed the ark of the covenant from

David's tabernacle, covered it, and marched it over to the Temple of Solomon, where they placed it in the Holy of Holies, back behind curtains again. This may seem like a step backward, but I am sure there is a plan here.

Solomon held a marvelous dedication service, and the presence of God came into the Temple of Solomon with such weight and heaviness that the trumpeters and everyone else who tried to minister fell under the power of the presence of God, just like they had in Moses' tabernacle (2 Chronicles 5:14).

Through the years, Solomon got off track. He began to marry foreign women who were involved in heathen worship. He did this to make foreign alliances and keep from going to war.

Eventually, Solomon married 700 wives and had 300 girlfriends. Can you imagine him trying to get into the shower through a jungle of a thousand pairs of pantyhose? The man was crazy!

THE ETHIOPIAN CONNECTION

The queen of Sheba came up from Ethiopia determined to meet this king she had heard so much about, and she was blown away by the magnificence of his kingdom and his wisdom.

History tells us that they either got married or had an affair, and they had a son. Two or three names are given for him. The historian Josephus wrote that when he came to see his father, he, too, was overwhelmed. It is said he asked repeatedly, "May I have the ark of God's presence?"

He reportedly took it back to Ethiopia with him. Lester Sumrall, a good friend of mine, used to preach on this. He said, "No one has seen the ark since, and no one knows where the ark of God is — except God and Marilyn Hickey." She had just written a book about the ark being in Ethiopia.

From the time of Solomon until Jesus came, there was no central focus of the presence of God in Israel. Jeremiah, Isaiah, Nehemiah — and the major and minor prophets — were always trying to bring Israel back into relationship with God. But there didn't seem to be a habitation for Him.

As God once said to me, "I really didn't live with them; I visited them. I would speak thunderously through the prophet's words and their mouths, and I would call them back to Me."

The children of Israel lived in terrible bondage and captivity under the Egyptians, the Babylonians, and the Syrians, because they were in such disobedience to Almighty God.

To summarize, after Solomon's reign, when the ark was no longer present, there never seems to have been a focal point for the national presence of God in Israel.

HIS PRESENCE IS IN US

Did you know that when Jesus came, He came first to the house of Israel, and He became the presence of God on earth? Today there are millions of us who carry His presence inside us. Today we are coming into a deeper dimension of God's presence, both individually and corporately, and the presence of God is literally going to dwell in us. There will be no lack or sadness in us — and I am not referring to the future millennial age; I am referring to the nasty "here and now."

In the presence of Jehovah, God Almighty, hearts are mended and troubles vanish. Jesus is coming back for that very reason.

When I was last in Israel, I was standing in my hotel room, looking out across the city of Jerusalem.

It was raining. God began to talk to me. He said, "I'm winding this thing up."

I love Israel, and I love the Jews. I try to go there every year, but I'm not going in the year 2000, because every nut in the universe is going to be in Jerusalem then. And we don't even know if the calendars are accurate.

I was weeping as I stood in my hotel room. That day I had been talking to an Israeli scholar about the rebirth of the Hebrew language. He said, "You know, after the dispersion of the Jews in 70 A.D., when we went all over the world, we nearly lost our Hebrew language.

He continued, "There was a rabbi and scholar named Eleazar Ben-Yehuda living in Israel. God put it in his heart to revive the Hebrew language, and he began to write books and to teach about the Hebrew language, updating the ancient language into the modern age."

CLEAR AND PURE SPEECH

Every year the Israelis come up with anywhere from 1500 to 3000 new words in Hebrew — words like "satellite," "airplane," "TV," and other modern terms. It is commonly said that if King David were to walk the streets of Jerusalem today, he would understand the Hebrew that is spoken, because it is basically ancient Hebrew!

Now come with me to the Book of Zephaniah. God led me to Zephaniah 3:9: "For then [changing their impure language] I will give to the people a clear and pure speech from pure lips..." That prophecy has been fulfilled in the last 50 years!

Verse 9 continues, "...that they may all call upon the name of the Lord, to serve Him with one unanimous consent and one united shoulder [bearing the yoke of the Lord]."

I also want you to notice verse 10, because we have been mentioning the queen of Sheba. Verse 10 says: "From beyond the rivers of Cush or Ethiopia those who pray to Me, the daughter of My dispersed people, will bring and present My offering."

In 1991, 85,000 Ethiopian Jews returned to Israel in a military airlift. If you watched CNN, you saw it. They called it "Operation Solomon"!

Tears ran down my face as I watched those black Jews who came through the lineage of Solomon, Sheba, and their son get off the airplanes wearing their colorful African garb. Many knelt and kissed the ground of Israel.

Verse 10 — "From beyond the rivers of Cush or Ethiopia those who pray to Me, the daughter of My dispersed people will bring and present My offering" — was fulfilled in that 1991 airlift. Israeli military transports flew to Addis Abba, Ethiopia, and transported those 85,000 Jews to Israel.

There are few prophecies left to be fulfilled, but this was one of them!

GOOD NEWS FOR THE UNITED STATES

God's presence is literally going to permeate the Earth. So don't be discouraged about the United States of America. Kenneth Copeland gave a prophecy in July 1999, saying, "In two years from this very night, in July 2001 — mark it down on your calendars — you will not recognize the United States of America, because we will begin to walk in the anointing to which we have been called as a nation."

Our government will bow its knee to Jesus Christ. The presence of God will take over this planet from one end to the other. For one thing, the glory is coming back, and that means it is harvest time. We have a few years left, regardless of what some people are prophesying.

This nation is not going down — it's going over! And it is because there are believers here who would rather have the presence of God than their next breath.

GOD'S LIVING, ABIDING PRESENCE

I want His presence more than anything in the whole universe! I will pay any price. I will go anywhere. I will say what needs to be said by the Spirit of God so we may have His presence.

This time, it will be a living, abiding presence. It will no longer simply be a visitation; it will be a habitation for Almighty God.

We love the habitation of God's presence, and this is the generation that is going to have it! But we are not ready for it yet. We need to shape up, sanctify ourselves, and prepare a place for His presence.

After we get into the tent of God's presence and seek His face, we will become "portable arks" of His presence to take into the world!

FULL OF GOD

As the Israelites stood in front of David's tabernacle, they could only experience the exterior part of God's presence. But you and I — because our human spirits have been recreated in the very image of God — can contain His presence.

We are "new creations," according to Second Corinthians 5:17, and God is in us "wall to wall." In fact, the Word says in Colossians 2:9,10 that we are full of God the Father, Jesus the Son, and the Holy Spirit — and that's His presence.

As we have seen, in God's presence, there is peace, wholeness, no lack, perfect vision, and no distraction.

In His presence, enemies quake, tremble, and will not attack you. In His presence, wholeness comes, because there is no lack.

Those who are struggling with decisions, being led one way one minute and another way the next, need to realize that in God's presence there is perfect vision. Why? Because when you get in His presence, confusion dies.

Furthermore, in His presence, there is bread for today and bread for tomorrow, enough for you and your household.

DAVID SHARES HIS HEART

Psalm 132 came straight out of David's heart. There were 18 wide steps on the south side of the Temple, and David wrote 18 "songs of ascent" to correspond to these steps that led up to the Temple.

Pilgrims would pause on each step and meditate on the faithfulness of God as they were going up into God's presence.

In Psalm 132:1-13, David wrote:

Lord, [earnestly] remember to David's credit all his humiliations and hardships and endurance.

How he swore to the Lord, and vowed to the mighty God of Jacob,

Surely I will not enter my dwelling house, or get into my bed,

I will not permit my eyes to sleep, or my eyelids to slumber,

Until I have found a place for the Lord, a habitation for the Mighty One of Jacob.

Lo, at Ephratah we [first] heard of [the discovered ark]; we found it in the fields of the wood — at [Kiriath-] Jearim.

Let us go into His tabernacle; let us worship at His footstool.

Arise, O Lord, to Your resting place, You and the ark [the symbol] of Your strength.

Let Your priests be clothed with righteousness [right living and right standing with God], and let Your saints shout for joy!

For Your servant David's sake turn not away the face of Your anointed and reject not Your own king.

The Lord swore to David in truth; He will not turn back from it; Of the fruit of your body [that's Jesus] I will set upon your throne.

If your children will keep My covenant and My testimony that I shall teach them, their children aso shall sit upon your throne for ever.

For the Lord has chosen Zion; He has desired it for His habitation.

That is you! You are the Church. You have been chosen by God. He has desired the Church for His habitation; for His resting place forever. When you get into His powerful presence, there is no lack of finances. You can be assured of this: Money is coming! Huge provision is coming! However, it is not coming to make us arrogant and silly; it is coming to enable us to take the Gospel to the ends of the Earth — and to take this "portable ark of His presence" to a world that is dying without it.

CHAPTER 8

A PLACE OF INTIMACY

David's tabernacle was a place of intimacy. There was neither form nor ritual there. Sacrifices were made only once, at the time when the ark of the covenant was first moved inside.

After those initial sacrifices, David's tabernacle was a place of total spontaneous worship before Almighty God. What happened was not practiced, it was not a ritual, and the priests didn't get up and announce the program.

This spontaneous worship before Almighty God included dancing and singing the song of the Lord. The tabernacle was also a place where the prophetic was as normal as breathing.

Praise and worship continued day and night. The Jews were in God's presence — they flowed in and out of His presence — all day long.

On the other hand, Gibeon, three and a half miles away, was the site where the old Mosaic tabernacle was located. The old order of priesthood was still there.

David, however, had an absolute revelation of grace, and he allowed people to stand in front of the Davidic tabernacle with naked faces, as it were, in the presence of God — faces veiled by their praise and worship, which acted as protection from the consuming fire of Almighty God.

David and Moses are spoken of more than any other individuals in the Old Testament, and both had an intense craving for the presence of God.

David discussed this in Psalm 26:8. Remember, we are studying habitation, not visitation.

The Amplified Bible translates this verse, "Lord, I love the habitation of Your house, and the place where Your glory dwells."

This is something we can do right now. We don't have to be in our glorified bodies to attain this. Remember, David wasn't even a "new creation" like we are.

A PSALM ABOUT GOD'S PRESENCE

The next Psalm is all about God's presence. In Psalm 27:1, David asked:

The Lord is my light and my salvation, whom shall I fear or dread?"

There will never be fear in God's presence.

...The Lord is the refuge and stronghold of my life; of whom shall I be afraid?

...Though a host encamp against me, my heart shall not fear....

Psalm 27:1,3

Did you know there is a host camped against you in the devil's camp? Some of them masquerade as believers, and they criticize and judge you. They will try to put you under condemnation, and they will do everything in their power to spoil the anointing on your life.

But David continued in verse 3:

...though war arise against me, (even then) in this will I be confident.

All of us who have been in the ministry very long have had our share of "wars" — some in our families and some among our dear friends.

DAVID'S SECRET

The second point in this Psalm is that there is confidence in the presence of the Lord and boldness to do His will. Note verse 4. It is David's secret — the one thing that David wanted more than anything else — the ultimate that he was requiring of God:

One thing have I asked of the Lord, that will I seek after, inquire for and [insistently] require, that I may dwell in the house of the Lord [in His presence] all the days of my life....

As David got further into verse 4, it makes you want to weep:

...to behold and gaze upon the beauty [the sweet attractiveness and the delightful loveliness] of the Lord, and to meditate, consider and inquire in His temple.

For in the day of trouble, He will hide me in His shelter; in the secret place of His tent [the tent of His presence] will He hide me. He will set me high upon a rock.

And now shall my head be lifted up above my enemies round about me; in His tent I will offer sacrifices and shouting of joy; I will sing, yes, I will sing praises to the Lord.

Psalm 27:4-6

Here David was talking about the sacrifice of praise. David was not big into blood sacrifices, but he was big into praise sacrifices.

God said, "He is a man after My own heart." Yet David was an adulterer, planned a murder, and saw to it that it was carried out. Isn't that amazing?

DEALING WITH THE MOCKING SPIRIT

God does not remember your past, and He gets irritated if you keep confessing the same old sins over and over again. He has thrown those sins into the sea of forgetfulness.

Now you must allow the Holy Spirit to erase out of your life negative experiences that haunt you.

They come from a mocking spirit, a spirit of Ishmael.

When Ishmael was a young man and Isaac was only a child, Sarah looked out the window one day and saw Ishmael taunting and mocking Isaac. And she said, "Abraham, they've got to go."

The Ishmaels — the mistakes of your life — will haunt you, scorn you, and keep you from obtaining God's fullness in your life unless you believe in the miracle side of Isaac, walk away from the haunting, mocking, scorning spirit, and cast the Ishmaels away from you.

God doesn't care what you were once; it's what you can be today through Him that matters — and that comes from being in the tent of His presence. Isn't that awesome?

I almost said what Moses said when God was setting me back in ministry: "God, have You looked at my resume lately?"

I threw out the baby with the bathwater. I wanted to get away from anything that smacked of church. I wanted to run as far as I could from religious folks.

THE WORST PAIN

I went through a divorce, which I believe is the worst pain an adult can ever go through. It is a living death, because you never bury the corpse.

So I said, "God, I can't go back into the ministry."

My parents and I had lived a very legalistic life, and I'm grateful for it. I couldn't go to the movies, and I didn't dare think about drinking alcohol.

I thought, "Lord, I've given you all these years, so now I'm going to party and have a good time."

The first thing I wanted to do was to go to a party with someone and drink alcohol, but I'd been so sheltered, I didn't even know what to order.

My mother was praying for me. She is such a pray-er, I could have only one drink. The second drink I threw up on everyone, and they never invited me back, so my party life was short-lived.

I found that you can't go to hell when three generations of people are praying for you in the Holy Ghost. It's impossible!

So I said, "God, have you read my resume? I don't think I can stand up and teach people anymore."

And He said, "What are you taking about?"

I had confessed all my sins. They were under the blood of Jesus. I hadn't lost my salvation. My former church thought I should get saved every Sunday night, but God didn't. I knew I was born again and on my way to heaven — and no one was going to steal that.

The Healing Begins

Then something glorious happened. I began to pray in the Holy Spirit and allow God to go into my innermost being and pray out the hurts of that betrayal and divorce.

When I went into that place with the Holy Spirit, I didn't know what I was praying all the time. But I was getting healed as I prayed in the Spirit, because the Word says that the Holy Spirit searches our hearts.

Then Paul, in First Corinthians 14:2, tells us that the Holy Spirit prays out mysteries:

> **For one who speaks in an [unknown] tongue speaks not to men but to God, for no one understands or catches his meaning, because in the (Holy) Spirit he utters secret truths and hidden things [not obvious to the understanding].**

Did you know you can hurt so bad, you can't verbalize it? You don't even have words for it, yet it's all inside you.

The Holy Spirit would shine that big spotlight [of His] down inside me, and I would pray in the Spirit, because Paul said that we are praying beyond our understanding when we pray that way.

I'm so healed, it's unbelievable! The father of my children is now a good friend. He remarried, and they moved out of town and had two children. He has a wonderful church in New Mexico.

MARVELOUS DISCOVERIES

I embarked on a journey to find out exactly what I did to get healed over our divorce. That's when God began to give me all this marvelous information on what happens when you pray in the Holy Ghost.

When God began to set me back into this ministry, and I didn't think I was worthy, He said, "I don't know what you're talking about. Your sins are under the blood."

Don't ever allow any kind of a mocking spirit to stop you from what God has called you to do. I don't care if you've had an abortion. I don't care if you've had 15 divorces. I don't care what kind of life you've lived.

The blood of Jesus is stronger than any mistake you've ever made, and through it you can be victorious in any situation in your life.

A DEVOTIONAL PSALM

David wrote Psalm 27 after he messed up his life by committing adultery with Bathsheba. I messed up a few times, but I didn't murder anyone, like David did. I wanted to, but I didn't. David began planning the murder of Bathsheba's husband when she told David she was carrying his child.

There are 14 verses in this Psalm. I suggest you read it from *The Amplified Bible* in your devotions every morning. Reading about God's presence in Psalm 27 will change your life! It has been one of the Psalms I have lived in for the last year.

In verse 6, David wrote:

> **And now shall my head be lifted up above my enemies round about me; in His tent I will offer sacrifices and shouting of joy....**

Do you know what that means? He wasn't holding his head down. He had no shame and no scorn. Shame ends right away when you get into praise and worship!

Verse 8 continues:

> **You have said, Seek you My face — inquire for and require My presence [as your vital need]. My heart says to You, Your face [Your presence], Lord, will I seek....**

If you study this in the Hebrew, it means "presence" or "face."

"THE LORD WILL ADOPT ME"

Verses 9-12 say:

> **Hide not Your face from me; turn not Your servant away in anger, You who have been my help!**

> **...Although my father and my mother have forsaken me, yet the Lord will take me up [adopt me as His child.**

> **Teach me Your way, O Lord, and lead me in a plain and even path because of my enemies — those who lie in wait for me.**

> Give me not up to the will of my adversaries; for false witnesses have risen against me; they breathe out cruelty and violence.

There are instructions, direction, and divine plans that God will reveal to you in His presence.

I love what David says in verse 13. I like to personalize it for myself this way: "What would have become of you, Louise, had you not believed that you would see the Lord's goodness in the land of the living!" Oh, hallelujah, I believed His Word, and His Word set me free!

Verse 14 concludes Psalm 27 with these words:

> Wait and hope for and expect the Lord; be brave and of good courage, and let your heart be stout and enduring.

Yes, wait and hope for and expect the Lord. It is awesome when we study about God's presence!

A SILENT PERIOD BEGINS

One of God's silent periods began in the Book of Malachi. It lasted for 400 years. There were little flickering flames seen through these 400 years, including the activities of the Maccabees, Jewish zealots, but there was no strong prophetic word from God.

The book ends, however, with this wonderful promise in Malachi 4:5,6:

> Behold, I will send you Elijah the prophet before the great and terrible day of the Lord comes.
>
> And He shall turn [and reconcile] the hearts of the [estranged] fathers to the [ungodly] children, and the hearts of the [rebellious] children to the [piety of] their fathers [a reconciliation produced by repentance of the ungodly]....

Then absolute silence reigned for the 400 years between the Old and New Testaments. There was nothing worth writing about, or the Holy Spirit would have written about it. There was nothing but silence from God.

CHAPTER 9

TRACING THE MANIFESTED PRESENCE OF GOD

There had not been a prophet in Israel for 400 years until the first chapter of Matthew. Now in the spirit and power of Elijah there sprang on the scene a wonderful, awesome young man. He was born by a miracle, born as an answer to the covenant, and he was called John the Baptist. He was surely born supernaturally, because his parents Zachariah and Elizabeth had been barren.

Then, suddenly, an angel visited them. Elizabeth was healed, and her womb was able to conceive. She bore John the Baptist, and he was something!

He ministered out in the wilderness, and he was a bit strange. He wore funny clothes and hair shirts, and he ate a strict vegetarian diet: wild honey and "locusts." No, he didn't eat insects, like everyone thinks; he ate beans from locust trees.

He preached boldly and forcefully — he didn't care who was in the congregation. He called sin, sin. And he was not too popular. Genuine prophets aren't popular with the world, because we tell it too straight, and religious folks hate us. Forgive them, Lord. They should love us, because we are really neat people!

History tells us that through John's ministry, one million people were baptized into the baptism of repentance. They weren't born again — they were born Jews under the Law — and now they were baptized into repentance. Although they were not new creations before the cross, their baptism marked an unprecedented beginning of a brand-new age.

THE PRESENCE OF GOD ON EARTH!

And into this electrified atmosphere came the Lord Jesus Christ, the presence of God on earth! God was still looking for a habitation, not a visitation.

Jesus was the Son of God and the son of man, yet human, and He brought the very essence of the Godhead upon the earth.

Continuing to follow the presence of God through Scripture, come with me to the Gospel of John. I have studied the disciples, and John called himself "The Beloved." He wrote the Book of John in the third person, because he thought that was being humble.

In actuality, he was just as immature as Peter! They were at each other's throats most of the time. John wrote of himself, "One of His disciples whom Jesus loved — whom He esteemed and delighted in — was reclining [next to Him] on Jesus' bosom" (John 13:23).

Jesus loved all His disciples. John drove Peter nuts with this third-person stuff about how he was Jesus' favorite.

THE WORD TABERNACLED AMONG US

In John 1:11-14, John wrote of Jesus:

He came to that which belonged to Him — to His own [domain, creation, things, world] — and they who were His own did not receive Him and did not welcome Him.

But to as many as did receive and welcome Him [this presence of God], He gave the authority [power, privilege, right] to become the children of God, that is, those who believe in — adhere to, trust in and rely on — His name;

> **Who owe their birth [the new birth] neither to bloods, nor to the will of the flesh [that of a natural father], but to God. — They are born of God!**
>
> **And the Word [Christ] became flesh (human, incarnate) and tabernacled — fixed His tent of flesh, lived awhile — among us; and we [actually] saw His glory....**

We can trace the manifested presence of God from the Garden of Eden to Mount Sinai and on into New Testament times. When John related this, he said, "And we saw His presence. We saw the presence of God." He was referring to what happened on the Mount of Transfiguration.

He wrote, "...and we [actually] saw His glory...such glory as an only begotten son receives from his father, full of grace (favor, loving kindness) and truth" (verse 14).

PETER'S TESTIMONY

Peter wrote about this same experience in Second Peter 1:16, stating, "For we were not following out cleverly devised stories when we made known to you the power and coming of our Lord Jesus Christ, the Messiah, but we were eyewitnesses of His majesty — grandeur, authority of sovereign power."

Did you know that you are in the same Church as Peter and John? After the Day of Pentecost, we came into the Church, and our names are on the same Church roll as Peter and John's. They were the first of the first fruits, and we came later.

If they were eyewitnesses — not just of Jesus' flesh but also of His glory — you and I are going to see with our own eyes the visible manifestations of the glory of God!

We will see it in signs, wonders, miracles, clouds, and pillars of fire. We will see awesome displays of the presence of God in this generation if we stay in the tent of His presence.

PETER REPORTS ON THE TRANSFIGURATION

Peter wrote further in verse 17:

> **For when He was invested [at the Transfiguration] with honor and glory from God the Father and a voice was borne to Him by the (splendid) Majestic Glory [in the bright cloud that overshadowed Him saying], This is My beloved Son in Whom I am well pleased and delight.**

John said, "We actually saw His glory." And Peter stated in verse 18, "We [actually] heard this voice borne out of heaven, for we were together with Him on the holy mountain." Notice their eyewitness testimonies involve two of the five senses.

Peter continued in verse 19:

> **And we have the prophetic Word [made] firmer still. You will do well to pay close attention to it as to a lamp shining in a dismal (squalid and dark) place, until the day breaks through [the gloom] and the Morning Star rises (comes into being) in your heart.**

The written Word of God always takes precedence over any kind of a manifestation. Everything must line up with this Book, or don't you believe it. Stay with the Word.

Peter discussed this in verses 20 and 21:

> **[Yet] first [you must] understand this, that no prophecy of Scripture is [a matter] of any personal or private or special interpretation (loosening, solving).**

For no prophecy ever originated because some man willed it [to do so] — it never came by human impulse — but as men spoke from God who were borne along (moved and impelled) by the Holy Spirit.

THE RESURRECTION CHAPTER

Returning to the Book of John, let's trace this through. The Book of John is quite clear on how God's presence came.

In John 20, Jesus had been crucified, buried, raised from the dead, and now He was about to appear to His disciples. This is "The Resurrection Chapter," where Jesus appeared to Mary Magdalene and began to have some interchange with His disciples, as in verse 19:

Then that same first day of the week, when it was evening, though the disciples were behind closed doors for fear of the Jews, Jesus came and stood among them, and said, Peace to you!

In Jesus' presence there is no fear. You won't fear the New Millennium, government regulations, or anything else in His presence. The disciples met together in fear, but watch what happened!

When Jesus walked in the room, the first words out of His mouth were, "Peace to you!" Remember, God said to Moses, "My presence shall go with you, and you shall have rest," which is part of peace. There is peace in His presence.

THE JOY OF SEEING JESUS

There is also great joy, as we see in verse 20:

So saying, He showed them His hands and His side. And when the disciples saw the Lord they were filled with joy (delight, exultation, ecstacy, rapture).

I love this! Did you know Jesus walked right through the wall in His glorified body? Think of all the fun we're going to have in the Millennial Age!

In this wonderful "catching up" or Rapture of the Church in midair, we're going to be changed and be just like Jesus. That's what the Word tells us. Paul gave us the wonderful revelation that we are going to be just like Jesus.

Brother Lester Sumrall preached a wonderful sermon on this. He said, "We're all going to be 33 years of age."

I embellish it a little. I say all you women are going to lose your cellulite, and all you guys are going to get your hair back. We're going to be glorious, glamorous creatures when we go up to meet Jesus in the air.

The Millennial Age will be awesome. We'll be just like Jesus! We'll walk through walls and scare the daylights out of all the natural people who are hanging around on earth, because there will be a bunch of them here.

Paul said we have an absolute guarantee that this vile body will be changed into immortality, and we shall be like Jesus.

TRAVELING IN OUR GLORIFIED BODIES

If we want to go through a wall, we'll just go through the wall. Instead of taking several flights to reach someplace like Baltimore, in my glorified body I'm simply going to say, "Baltimore" — and I'll be there in Nordstrom's. If the millennium is a perfect place, it will have Nordstrom's, or at least Bloomingdale's — right, ladies?

One of my favorite places to visit is the island of Maui. I've asked the Lord, "When we get our glorified bodies, may I please build a church on Maui?" I won't have to ride airplanes six hours from Los Angeles to get there. I'll just say, "Maui," and I'll be there. That's awesome!

I once asked Jesus about our scars, because I went through a barbed wire fence when I was about 6, and I've got a leg with three big scars on it. So I asked, "Jesus, in going up, can I get a leg that doesn't have scars?"

He told me, "Absolutely. I only kept Mine for proof. I showed My hands and My side." When He did, the disciples knew it was the Lord. He proved to them that that's who He was, and they were filled with joy. They were in His presence, and "In the presence of the Lord is fullness of joy." They must have breathed a collective sigh of relief to be with the Master once again.

JESUS COMMISSIONS HIS DISCIPLES

After Jesus greeted the disciples, He commissioned them, as He had in John chapters 13 through 19. I teach on "The Pathway to Power" and "Attitudes, Ethics, and Motivation" out of those chapters.

John records in John 20:21,22:

> **Then Jesus said to them again, Peace to you! [Just] as the Father has sent Me forth, so I am sending you.**
>
> **And having said this, He breathed on [them] and said to them, Receive (admit) the Holy Spirit!**

In verse 22, the disciples became new creations — all 10 of them. There weren't 12 anymore, because Judas was dead. The betrayer had gone and hung himself because he had violated the salt covenant.

Also, Thomas was not there. It was Wednesday night, his bowling night, so there were only 10 disciples present. This group had been together for three and a half years, but one member didn't come to church on one of the most important nights of the ministry's history.

Although the disciples became the first new creations, they didn't speak in tongues until the Book of Acts, but they were regenerated when they were breathed on by Jesus. His presence came on the inside of them in that very moment.

Now there was no longer just one person walking the earth manifesting the presence of God; there were 10, and they were living in physical bodies. Jesus was the only one living in a glorified body.

THE IMPORTANCE OF FAITHFULNESS

I hope you're paying attention to this. God requires absolute faithfulness, and if pastors don't preach faithfulness to their people, they're doing them an injustice. No, you shouldn't berate people and all that, but you must teach faithfulness.

I'm not kidding you — "the ball of fire," so to speak, is going to come down the middle aisle some Wednesday night or some Sunday night during the Super Bowl.

We're all going to get an awesome infusion of power, but you guys holding footballs and bowling balls will wonder what happened.

Some use their kids as an excuse. They use schools and school activities, claiming their kids must be in bed by 8 o'clock.

I excelled in almost everything throughout high school and college, and I had to be in church every time the doors opened!

My mother was tone deaf and my dad couldn't keep time, so they made sure I could sing and play. I started music lessons when I was 6, and when I was

11, I could play the piano in three keys — so we sang every song in the book in those three keys.

I had to be in church regardless of rain, shine, school plays, and so forth, because my parents instilled in me that the work of God comes before anything else in our lives.

When I see people who forsake the assembling of themselves together in church, I think, "God, shake them until their teeth rattle!" You must understand that the most important thing you do is to assemble with God's believers.

REMAIN WITH YOUR OWN COMPANY

In the Book of Acts, believers returned to their own company every time they had been beaten and thrown in jail. Stay with your roots and your own company. Don't leave the faith crowd.

There are other people preaching good things, but it isn't as good as this. This is what set us free; this is what set us on the road to victory; this is what set us on the road to God's presence.

You won't hear teaching like we have in the faith camp in anyone else's camp. So stay with your roots; stay with your company; stay with the people who understand you.

As we saw, Thomas wasn't present when Jesus visited His disciples, and when he did show up, he was full of doubt. Pastors, do you know who will criticize your last good service? It's the people who weren't there. That's right — they'll criticize it every time.

I once told some of my people, "Old Brother So-and-so got healed of cancer last night!"

They responded, "Well, we'll see."

They weren't there.

Old Brother So-and-so did get healed of cancer. He had a huge tumor, and he had been treated at the cancer center in Tucson. When I put my hand on the tumor and prayed, it felt like a baseball. That thing melted right under my hand, and I shouted the victory! This elderly man was not only totally healed; he lived for another 10 years and died of a heart attack.

Doubting Thomas and His Friends

Yet there are always people who say, "Well, we'll see." Because they weren't in the service when the miracle happened, they always interject doubt.

But Thomas, one of the twelve, called the Twin, was not with them when Jesus came.

John 20:24

You pastors should preach faithfulness. You could preach on verse 24 for a long time. And members of your congregation who attended on Wednesday nights should start calling those who weren't there early on Thursday morning, saying, "Guys, you should have heard what the pastor said last night! No, we're not going to tell you, but it was awesome. He exposed some important truths, and if you guys had been there, you would have known everything." Make it sound good!

This is what the other disciples did to Thomas. They kept saying, "We have seen the Lord! His presence came into the room!"

Thomas Holds Out

But Thomas stubbornly replied, "...Unless I see in His hands the mark made by the nails, and put my finger into the nail prints, and put my hand into His side, I will never believe it."

The other disciples had the presence of God

within them, but Thomas had to go without the presence of God for eight days. Don't tell me he wasn't jealous; he was. He thought, "I am such a fool! I should have been there!"

There is no record of where Thomas was, so it must not have been important. He could have been fishing, hunting, or something like that.

Eight days later, the disciples were again in the house, and Thomas was with them. I guess so! I wouldn't have let them out of my sight! I would have been like Elisha with Elijah. I would have said, "I'm staying with you guys. I'm going to see Jesus the next time."

Even though they were behind closed doors, Jesus came right through the wall. I imagine Thomas' eyes bugged out of his head. Jesus said, "Peace to you!" I'm sure in eight days' time, those 10 guys had retold this story so often, it was greatly embellished.

I love it when preachers get together. They keep adding one sentence after another. It's not lying; it's just embellishing everything God does. We used to call it "evangelastically speaking." That means we elasticize stories like this.

JESUS REBUKES THOMAS

Jesus challenged Thomas in verse 27:

Thomas, Reach out your finger here and see My hands; and put out your hand and place [it] in My side. Do not be faithless and incredulous, but [stop your unbelief] and believe!

Thomas replied, "My Lord and my God!" because the presence of God was so strong in the room.

> **Jesus said to him, Because you have seen
> Me, Thomas, do you now believe (trust, have
> faith)?**

That was a reprimand, and Thomas was chastised. Jesus then continued in verse 29, pronouncing this blessing:

> **Blessed and happy and to be envied are
> those who have never seen Me, and yet have
> believed and adhered to and trusted in and
> relied on Me.**

Put your hand on your heart and confess: "Father, I am blessed, for I believe in Jesus. I haven't seen Him physically, but I have seen Him by the Spirit, and I am blessed."

Verse 30 concludes:

> **There are also many other signs and miracles, which Jesus performed in the presence
> of the disciples, which are not written in this
> book.**

CHAPTER 10

GOD'S PRESENCE IN THE CHURCH

The Church was birthed on the Day of Pentecost, according to Acts 2. You know the story.

In the first chapter of Acts, Jesus' 11 disciples were in the Upper Room with other people, including women who followed Jesus.

Jews did not worship alongside women, so the women were congregated in one section of the room. They were determined they were not going to be denied the promised blessing, whatever it was.

Pastors, here is the second point in your message on faithfulness.

According to Paul, more than 500 eyewitnesses saw Jesus after His resurrection (1 Corinthians 15:6), but only 120 showed up on Wednesday night in the Upper Room. Isn't that amazing?

They didn't know what they were expecting, because Jesus had simply said, "Go and wait." Waiting is not fun. We're all impatient, and they were, too.

I can see Peter, who was the most impatient, pacing around the room, grumbling, "Lord, how much longer will we have to wait? We've been in here nine days, almost 10, and these women are getting on my nerves! You know we don't allow women to sit next to us in our religious meetings, and this is a funny-looking bunch. Besides, I'm not sure of what we're waiting for."

THE CHURCH'S BIRTHDAY

All of a sudden, the Spirit of God spoke up on

the inside of Peter and said, "Peter, would you read a Psalm that says there will be one elected to take Judas' place?"

So Peter announced, "Folks, wait a minute! We're not doing something right. We're not in order yet."

The number of God's government order is 12. Throughout the Gospels, the Word speaks of the 12 thrones, the 12 tribes, and the 12 apostles.

And that is how Matthias happened to be put in place as the twelfth foundational stone of the building God is building, using us as "lively stones." (See Acts 1:15-26.)

Instantly, everything was complete! Order was established, because 12 is the number of God's government. Suddenly, there came the sound of a rushing mighty wind, and the Upper Room was shaken!

This was the reality of the symbolism played out in Exodus 19, when Mount Sinai shook, fire fell, smoke descended, lightning flashed, and a trumpet sounded — only this time the sound of the trumpet was 120 people speaking in tongues!

FILLED WITH THE POWER

They were new creations now, filled with the power of the Holy Spirit. That infilling instantly stopped the competition between Peter and John. It stopped the anguish of those who worried that they would not be recognized. It totally dissipated any kind of competition between believers, because now all were new creations, and each had his or her own portion of the Holy Spirit. You will notice that John didn't say, "Now, Peter, it's my turn to preach, so don't you get up here and preach."

Peter went down into the street outside and began to preach to the crowd that had gathered. He said, "Folks, these people are not drunk like you think," and then he gave a marvelous exposition from the Scriptures, beginning in Joel.

He explained — because that's what teachers do — the supernatural infilling of the Holy Spirit, tracing it to Joel's prophecy, setting it in its right place.

PORTABLE "ARKS OF THE COVENANT"

Now there was no longer just one person named Jesus, and there were no longer just 12 men called His disciples — now there were 120 people who were walking, portable "arks of the covenant," full of the presence of God.

And the outward sign of that inward work was tongues!

The Church was birthed in the sound of a rushing mighty wind, and 3000 people were born again that day.

Let me remind you, God married the Jews in Exodus 19, and Jesus married us in Acts 2! We are the Bride of Christ — we are even the Body of Christ — and we are the ones who are full of the Holy Spirit. The presence of God dwells with us corporately and individually.

When we come together, there is a multiplication of anointing; a multiplication of His presence. We all bring our parts of the anointing to church, and together we have a multiplication of the presence of Almighty God.

When God's tent of presence covers the congregation, anything you may have need of is met in His presence!

PAUL'S GLORIOUS REVELATION

When the apostle Paul came along, he had a glorious revelation of the Church, and he wrote about it.

He said, "Now, then, we are all temples of the Holy Spirit. We are wall-to-wall Spirit of God."

Don't go another five seconds without His presence! Come into my tent, and I will share some scriptures that will show you how to get into the tent of God's presence.

In Galatians 1, Paul rehearsed how he got into the tent of God's presence. This is so new, it's "hot off the press."

Paul was a bit aggravated that the Galatians were turning away from the truth. In verses 11 and 12, he addressed his Jewish brethren who were returning to legalism:

> **For I want you to know, brethren, that the Gospel which was proclaimed and made known by me is not man's gospel — a human invention, according to or patterned after any human standard.**

> **For indeed I did not receive it from man, nor was I taught it; [it came to me] through a [direct] revelation [given] by Jesus Christ, the Messiah.**

SET APART

Then Paul told these people about the tent of God's presence in verses 13-16:

> **You have heard of my earlier career and former manner of life in the Jewish religion (Judaism)...**

> **And [have heard how] I outstripped many of the men of my own generation among the people of my race, in [my advancement in study and observance of the laws of] Judaism, so extremely enthusiastic and zealous I was for the traditions of my ancestors.**

> **But when He Who had chosen and set me apart [even] before I was born, and had called me by His grace...**
>
> **Saw fit and was pleased to reveal (unveil, disclose) His Son within me** [Paul had found the tent of His presence!] **so that I might proclaim Him among the Gentiles...as the glad tidings, immediately I did not confer with flesh and blood — did not consult or counsel with any frail human beings or communicate with any one.**

Let me tell you something: When you stay in the tent of His presence, it is wonderful to have everything you've learned affirmed by the brothers around you — but if their approval is not forthcoming, stay in the tent of God's presence and let His presence give you direction.

In that case, you will not be led by signs, wonders, and prophecies; you will be led by God's Spirit and His Word.

PAUL'S ARABIAN YEARS

Paul noted in Galatians 1:17-19:

> **Nor did I [even] go up to Jerusalem to those who were apostles — special messengers of Christ — before I was; but I went away and retired into Arabia, and afterward I came back again to Damascus.**
>
> **Then three years later, I did go up to Jerusalem to become (personally) acquainted with Cephas (Peter), and remained with him for fifteen days.**
>
> **But I did not see any of the other apostles — the special messengers of Christ — except James the brother of our Lord.**

The wilderness is where Paul found the tent of God's presence. Three years later, he went up to

Jerusalem to become personally acquainted with the elders. Paul wanted to submit his ministry to them. This is so important. Pastors, get a pastor!

Brother Kenneth E. Hagin speaks into my life, and my son Bruce is my pastor. I pay my tithes to his church, and I know that God gives him directions for me, so I receive them.

I wouldn't go to my next meeting without a pastor; that's the way I am. I love to be submitted to leadership. Age has nothing to do with this in the Spirit.

JOURNEY TO JERUSALEM

It was while Paul was in the desert that he began to pray in tongues more than everyone else, and it was there that he discovered the tent of God's presence in his life. Paul described this time in his life in Galatians 2:1,2:

> Then after (an interval) of fourteen years I again went up to Jerusalem. [This time I went] with Barnabas, taking Titus along with [me] also.
>
> I went because it was specially and divinely revealed to me that I should go, and I put before them the Gospel, [declaring to them that] which I preach among the Gentiles. However, [I presented the matter] privately before those of repute, [for I wanted to make certain, by thus at first confining my communication to this private conference] that I was not running or had not run in vain — guarding against being discredited either in what I was planning to do or had already done.

Paul, after about 17 years of ministry and receiving these divine revelations when he was out in ministry and the wilderness and praying in tongues more than everyone else, still wanted to make sure that his doctrine was correct!

A PRIVATE VISIT

He said, in effect, "Privately I took my doctrine to the elders in Jerusalem, because I wanted them to judge my heart, to test my doctrine, and to see if what I was preaching lined up with their spirit, because I had been called to the Gentiles.

"I wanted them to know that God was now going to be bringing in the Gentiles, and I have been commissioned to preach to these people and to bring them into the Gospel.

"I convened with the elders privately, because I needed affirmation of what I had been shown — affirmation that I wasn't some lunatic out there in the desert getting stupid revelations."

You will never get so spiritual, so mature, and so perfected that you don't need input from your elders.

Submit your doctrines privately to the elders before you preach them publicly. This will keep you off dangerous ground. Not submitting doctrines to the judgment of others is how stupid doctrines, such as "manifested sons," get started.

I could name 15 false doctrines such as "manifested sons" that I have lived through three or four times. If the people who preach false doctrines would submit those doctrines privately to elders, they wouldn't teach them publicly, because they would have been corrected privately.

And if this was necessary for the apostle Paul, it is necessary for Louise Brock and you!

SUBMITTING TO THE ELDERS

I submit to my elders all the time. Recently, I've been talking to some friends about God's silence. If they have any input, I want it.

I don't want error in my life or doctrine. I don't want to teach or preach error. I don't want to live by error. I want to live by the Word of God and the truth of God.

As Peter pointed out, "...no prophecy of Scripture is [a matter] of any personal or private or special interpretation..." (2 Peter 1:20). That is why I submit myself and my doctrine to the elders all the time. I want to know if I'm on track or not.

Sometimes I go on trips with ministry friends. We sit around and preach to each other, and we add to each other's lives. Or we'll say, "Wow, I'm not so sure about that. It sounds like a windy doctrine."

HELP WITH DECISIONS

It's wonderful when you can sit with elders, like Paul did here. He said, "I did it. I presented this matter privately before those of repute." If you do this, it will "save your bacon" hundreds of times. And what you talk about needn't be limited to doctrine; you can submit decisions you want to make.

Paul said, "I wanted to make certain that I was not running or had not run in vain...But [all went well]."

Paul had discovered the tent of God's presence in the wilderness, and he lived in that tent. By that I mean that the presence of God was with Paul everywhere he went.

Paul began his letter to Timothy by saying (1 Timothy 1:2):

To Timothy, my true son in the faith: Grace...mercy and heart peace [be yours] from God the Father and Christ Jesus our Lord.

Then, starting in verse 3, he began to mentor Timothy, giving him practical advice.

"STAY WHERE YOU ARE"

As I urged you when I was on my way to Macedonia, stay on where you are at Ephesus in order that you may warn and admonish and charge certain individuals not to teach any different doctrine.

Timothy was a young man at this time. It is said his church at Ephesus could have had as many as 750,000 members. Paul advised, "Don't leave Ephesus. Stay where you are."

I've wanted to give up lots of times, and various people have spoken into my life, saying, "Don't move — don't give up — don't change." They saved me many heartaches and bad decisions.

Paul then gave Timothy some advice in verse 4 about certain people in his church:

> **Nor to give importance to or occupy themselves with legends (fables, myths) and endless genealogies which foster and promote useless speculations and questionings, rather than acceptance in faith of God's administration....**

IMPURE AND IMMORAL ISSUES

Starting in verse 10, Paul refers to impure and immoral persons, whoever

> **...is opposed to wholesome teaching and sound doctrine,**

> **As laid down by the glorious Gospel of the blessed God, with which I have been entrusted.**

> **I give thanks to Him Who has granted me (the needed) strength and made me able [for this], Christ Jesus our Lord, because He has judged and counted me faithful and trustworthy, appointing me to [this stewardship of] the ministry.**

> 1 Timothy 1:10-12

135

You see, it's Jesus' ministry, and we are stewards of it. He is the Head of the Church — the Chief Bishop — the Shepherd of our souls.

Paul continued giving thanks in verses 18,19, saying:

> This charge and admonition I commit in trust to you, Timothy, my son, in accordance with the prophetic intimations which I formerly received concerning you, so that inspired and aided by them you may wage the good warfare,
>
> Keeping fast hold on faith....

We are at an all-time low with faith in faith churches, and preachers need to prepare some good sermons on faith.

THREE CHARGES TO TIMOTHY

"Holding fast to the faith" is a charge. Paul said, "This charge and admonition I commit in trust to you." The first thing he committed to Timothy was the prophetic word that had been spoken over him.

The way you get in the tent of God's presence and stay there is by using such prophecies to pray over yourself, being encouraged by those words that were spoken over you.

The next thing was holding fast to the faith.

Prayer was the third thing Paul committed to Timothy. He gave him instructions about prayer in First Timothy 2:1-8, and in verses 3 and 8 he said:

> For such [praying] is good and right, [it is] pleasing and acceptable to God our Savior...
>
> I desire therefore that in every place men should pray, without anger or quarreling or resentment or doubt [in their minds], lifting up holy hands.

THE IMPORTANCE OF PURITY

Coming to chapter 3, you will find that it is all about purity. You will not be able to stay in the tent of His presence without purity in your heart.

Paul stressed the importance of purity in those holding such offices as bishops and deacons. This is the day when God is calling us to holiness!

You are going to have to get rid of the junk in your life. For example, we have people in our church whom we are counseling to get off the Internet, because pornography is such a temptation to them.

We have Internet access in our church computers because we use e-mail and so forth, but we have made it an absolute rule that if any of our employees is caught looking at pornography, he or she will be fired immediately. We will not tolerate it.

We as a society have been slowly inoculated to the point where we don't get indignant anymore with pornography or the unbelievably ungodly situations we see on television or read about in books, newspapers, and magazines.

We must draw a line in the sand of God's presence and declare, "People, if you come any closer with sin in your life, you will be incinerated on the spot, because God is a holy God, and He is going to have a holy people."

Otherwise, we are not going to be able to walk into this new generation with the tent of His presence. I don't know how to state it any stronger than that.

LOUSY ATTITUDES

We have been discussing overt sins, but just as serious is having a lousy attitude toward another minister or someone else's prosperity. This is also sin in the heart and mind of God.

You cannot minister purity and the presence of God while having a lousy attitude, because that is rebellion in its highest form. And it is so subtle, you could have that attitude and hardly know it.

When you return to your own quiet time, all of a sudden you will realize that the jealous words and opinions you have spoken reflect what is in your heart. Then you will realize it is none of your business when God brings prosperity to other people.

We don't know what seeds they have sown; we don't have any idea of the petitions they have made before God; and we don't know how big their vision is. Why, then, should we criticize what God is blessing them with?

I think it's wonderful, and I rejoice in every person's prosperity that comes from the hand of God.

A STANDARD OF CONDUCT

There is a standard of conduct for us. As we finish chapter 3, we find Paul telling Timothy about it:

> **If I am detained, you may know how people ought to conduct themselves in the household of God, which is the church of the living God...**
>
> **And great and important and weighty, we confess, is the hidden truth — the mystic secret — of godliness. He (God) was made visible in human flesh, justified and vindicated in the (Holy) Spirit, was seen by angels, preached among the nations, believed on in the world [and] taken up in glory.**
>
> **1 Timothy 3:15,16**

Then Paul wrote more practical advice to Timothy.

If you lay all these instructions before the brethren, you will be a worthy steward and a good minister of Christ Jesus, ever nourishing your own self on the truths of the faith and of the good [Christian] instruction which you have closely followed.

But refuse and avoid irreverent legends — profane and impure and godless fictions, mere grandmothers' tales — and silly myths [that means stupid doctrines and traditions], and express your disapproval of them. Train yourself toward godliness (piety) — keeping yourself spiritually fit.

For physical training is of some value...but godliness [spiritual training] is useful and of value in everything and in every way...

Continue to command these things and to teach them.

1 Timothy 4:6-8,11

All I want to be is a worthy steward and a good minister of Jesus Christ.

STAYING IN THE TENT

Don't sacrifice the tent of your individual presence with God for the tent of the corporate presence. You must have your personal prayer tent like Moses and Paul did before you can engineer the "big tent" of His presence over your congregations.

Paul used the whole book of First Timothy to give instructions on how to stay in the tent of God's presence. Paul erected a tent of His presence just like Moses prepared a tent in Exodus 33:11 for Joshua to stay in; and Paul wanted Timothy to stay in his tent.

"Until you become that man," Paul said, "stay in this tent. This is what you must do to stay in this tent." He added in First Timothy 4:13-15:

Till I come, devote yourself to [public and private] reading, to exhortation — preaching and personal appeals — and to teaching and instilling doctrine.

Do not neglect the gift which is in you, [that special inward endowment] which was directly imparted to you [by the Holy Spirit] by prophetic utterance when the elders laid their hands upon you [at your ordination].

Practice and cultivate and meditate upon these duties, throw yourself wholly into them [your ministry], so that your progress may be evident to everybody.

That is how you stay in the tent of His presence.

NO HALFWAY MEASURES

"Throw yourself wholly into them...so that your progress may be evident to everybody." I love that in *The Amplified Bible.* I've never done anything halfway myself. If I was going to sin, I wanted to sin. However, I chose to devote my life wholly to God, so I threw myself into serving God.

Do you have an *Amplified Bible*? I love it! It's the wordy women's Bible. Verse 16 says, "Look well to yourself (to your own personality)...." Personality is part of you. It's your soulish area that you are working on day by day. If you don't develop a pleasing, loving personality, you won't draw many people to the Lord.

Verse 16 in its entirety reads:

Look well to yourself (to your own personality) and to [your] teaching; persevere in these things — hold to them; for by so doing you will save both yourself and those who hear you.

First Timothy 5 deals with giving. Did you know if you're a stingy preacher, you're going to die a poor preacher? You are only increased by giving. Why? Because sowing and reaping is the law of God.

TAKING CARE OF WIDOWS

The proper treatment of widows is also mentioned. Do you know what we did in our church? We had an alms program that seemingly was as large as public welfare. Finally we smartened up and said, "All you able-bodied guys must work. From now on, we will help only the widows and the single mothers with children." So our alms program changed. We still give as much, but it is directed differently, because now we do it scripturally.

We printed cards to give to the men who beg on downtown street corners. Some of them hold signs stating they need work. We tell them we'll give them $10 an hour if they will report to the church, and we list some of the jobs they could do for us, such as painting and yard work. We're still waiting for the first one to show up!

These homeless men make between $200 and $300 a day begging in Tucson in the wintertime. With the printed card, we give them carfare to get to the church, but we have yet to see the first one come to work for $10 an hour. I've cleaned toilets at the church for free and still do!

DON'T BE PARTIAL

In First Timothy 5:21,22, Paul gives another charge:

> I solemnly charge you in the presence of God and of Christ Jesus and of the chosen angels, that you guard and keep [these rules] without personal prejudice or favor, doing nothing from partiality.

Do not be in a hurry in the laying on of hands — giving the sanction of the church too hastily [in reinstating expelled offenders or in ordination in questionable cases] — nor share or participate in another man's sins; keep yourself pure.

This is just the beginning on any study of the presence of God. After reading it, may you be full of God's presence — totally immersed in the tent of His presence!

ABOUT THE AUTHOR

Louise Brock is the founder of Faith Community Church in Tuscon, Arizona, where her son, Bruce Brock, now pastors. Following in her parents' footsteps, she has dedicated her life to ministering the uncompromised Word of God to the Body of Christ.

As a gifted teacher, Louise flows in a prophetic anointing teaching the truths of God's Word to enlighten and edify the Church of Jesus Christ and win souls for the kingdom with signs and wonders following.

Her depth of insight into the riches of wisdom found in the Old Testament challenges believers worldwide. She serves a full schedule of national and international ministry engagements every year, as well as fulfilling her office as Regional Representative for Faith Christian Fellowship International.

OTHER BOOKS BY LOUISE BROCK

HOW TO DEVELOP THE MIND OF CHRIST IN YOU

OFFENSES WILL COME
(HOW TO PROTECT YOUR HEART)

PROPHETIC PRAYER